First World War

and Army of Occupation

War Diary

France, Belgium and Germany

37 DIVISION
Divisional Troops
247 Machine Gun Company
16 July 1917 - 28 February 1918

WO95/2524/4

The Naval & Military Press Ltd
www.nmarchive.com
Published in association with The National Archives

Published by

The Naval & Military Press Ltd

Unit 10 Ridgewood Industrial Park,

Uckfield, East Sussex,

TN22 5QE England

Tel: +44 (0) 1825 749494

www.naval-military-press.com

www.nmarchive.com

This diary has been reprinted in facsimile from the original. Any imperfections are inevitably reproduced and the quality may fall short of modern type and cartographic standards.

Contents

Document type	Place/Title	Date From	Date To
Heading	WO95/2524/3 247th Machine Gun Coy July 1917. Feb 1918		
Miscellaneous	37th Division 247th Machine Gun Coy. Jly 1917 1918 Feb		
Heading	War Diary 247th Machine Gun Coy 37th Divn July 1917		
War Diary	Le Havre	16/07/1917	18/07/1917
War Diary	Buchy	19/07/1917	19/07/1917
War Diary	Abbeville	19/07/1917	19/07/1917
War Diary	Bailleul	19/07/1917	19/07/1917
War Diary	Camp	20/07/1917	31/07/1917
War Diary	Between Messines And Oosttaverne	31/07/1917	31/07/1917
Heading	War Diary 247 M.G. Coy Aug 1917 Vol 2		
War Diary	Between Messines and Oosttaverne	31/07/1917	07/08/1917
War Diary	Camp At N.31.d. 1.2.	08/08/1917	08/08/1917
War Diary	Pallas FM. N. 9.d. 7.8.	09/08/1917	11/08/1917
War Diary	Pallas Farm	12/08/1917	12/08/1917
War Diary	West Of Bug Wood	13/08/1917	16/08/1917
War Diary	Oosttaverne West Of Bug Wood. Rose Wood	16/08/1917	22/08/1917
War Diary	Damm Strasse	19/08/1917	20/08/1917
War Diary	West Of Bug Wood	22/08/1917	31/08/1917
Heading	War Diary 247th M.G. Coy Sept 1917 Vol 3		
War Diary	Palais Farm	01/09/1917	03/09/1917
War Diary	Line	04/09/1917	11/09/1917
War Diary	Line W. Of Battle Wood	11/09/1917	13/09/1917
War Diary	Palais Farm	14/09/1917	18/09/1917
War Diary	Line	18/09/1917	24/09/1917
War Diary	Palais Farm	25/09/1917	26/09/1917
War Diary	Berthen	27/09/1917	28/09/1917
War Diary	Line	29/09/1917	29/09/1917
Heading	War Diary 247 M.G. Coy Oct 1917 Vol 4		
War Diary	Line	01/10/1917	11/10/1917
War Diary	Transport Lines	12/10/1917	14/10/1917
War Diary	N15 b. 4.9.	15/10/1917	15/10/1917
War Diary	R 22. b. 7.5.	16/10/1917	31/10/1917
Miscellaneous	247 M.G.C. Training Programme for first Phase Of 9 days		
Miscellaneous	247 M.G.C. Programme Of Training		
Miscellaneous	Company Sports Events		
War Diary	Mt Kokereel R22.b 70.50	01/11/1917	08/11/1917
War Diary	Line	08/11/1917	31/12/1917
War Diary	Line E. of Hollebeke	01/01/1918	01/01/1918
War Diary	Line	02/01/1918	11/01/1918
War Diary	Barossa Camp & Move To Mill Fontaine	12/01/1918	14/01/1918
War Diary	Mill Fontaine	14/01/1918	31/01/1918
Miscellaneous	247. M.G. Coy. Programme Of Training 13-1-18 To 19-1-18		
Miscellaneous	247 M.G. Coy Programme of Training For The Period 20-1-18 To 26-1-18		

Miscellaneous	247 M.G. Coy Programme of Training For The Period 27-1-18 To 2.2.18		
War Diary	Mill Fontaine	01/02/1918	14/02/1918
War Diary	Line	15/02/1918	28/02/1918
Miscellaneous			

WO95/2524/3

247th MACHINE GUN COY

July 1917 - Feb 1918

37TH DIVISION

247TH MACHINE GUN COY.

JLY 1917-~~MAY 1919~~
1918 FEB

Vol I

War Diary

~~247th~~ 247th Machine Gun Coy

37th DIVN

JULY 1917

May '19

Instructions regarding War Diaries and Intelligence Summaries are contained in F. S. Regs., Part II. and the Staff Manual respectively. Title pages will be prepared in manuscript.

WAR DIARY
or
INTELLIGENCE SUMMARY.
(Erase heading not required.)

Army Form C. 2118.

Place	Date	Hour	Summary of Events and Information	Remarks and references to Appendices
LE HAVRE.	16-7-17	11.15am	Arrived 11.15 a.m. Detailed fatigue party to clean up the boat and stables after all animals and transport had been withdrawn. Marched to Rest Camp (No 1) and were allotted tents. Transport arrived at Camp at 3.25 p.m. Forwarded "Marching in" State and obtained a copy of Camp Standing Orders which was read to the NCOs + men on parade. Made arrangements for cooking.	ESC
do	17-7-17		Held Kit inspection and replaced deficiencies as far as possible. All ranks confined to Camp. All guns, spare parts etc cleaned. Transport cleaned. An A.S.C. Driver, G.S. limber and two Heavy Draft Horses taken on strength.	ESC
	18-7-17		Orders to move at night. During day the men were marched down to the beach, and bathed. Orders for move stated that the unit was to arrive at the GARE aux MARCHANDISES	ESC
		7.30 pm	at 7.30 p.m. Animals watered and entrained - transport entrained and finally the men.	
		9.32 pm	At 9.32 p.m. the train moved out of HAVRE and at 1.0 a.m. arrived at BUCHY where	
BUCHY	19-7-17	1.0 am	the animals were watered and hot tea made for the men who were awake.	ESC.
ABBEVILLE	19-7-17	9.40am	At 9.40 a.m. there was a stay of 40 minutes at ABBEVILLE. Here the animals were watered and fed, rations were issued to the men, hot tea was made and as many men as possible washed and shaved.	
			Next Stop - HAZEBROUCK. - a stay of 15 mins before continuing to	
BAILLEUL	19-7-17	5.20 pm	BAILLEUL. Here everything was detrained and made ready for immediate move. Were met by Divisional M.G. Officer and were informed we were attached to the 37th DIVISION. Marched to our Camp via DRANOUTRE. Under Canvas. Watered + fed animals — ... on picketing line.	

(A6092) Wt. W. 12839/M1293 750,000 1/17. D. D. & L., Ltd. Forms/C.2118/14.

* Instructions regarding War Diaries and Intelligence Summaries are contained in F. S. Regs., Part II. and the Staff Manual respectively. Title pages will be prepared in manuscript.

WAR DIARY
or
INTELLIGENCE SUMMARY.
(Erase heading not required.)

Army Form C. 2118.

Place	Date	Hour	Summary of Events and Information	Remarks and references to Appendices
CAMP	20-7-17		Visited by G.S.O.1. D.A.A.G. D.A.Q.M.G. D.A.D.V.S. D.A.D.O.S. A.D.M.S. Two Mules, exchanges at SOUTHAMPTON to be Malleined.	ERC
		4.0pm	Inspected by MAJOR. GENERAL. H.B. WILLIAMS. C.B., D.S.O. commanding 37th DIVISION.	
	21-7-17		Men paraded for Inspection by Medical Officer in charge of the Unit. Arrangements made by which 2 Officers and 36 men should go into the line with 112 M.G. Coy for Instruction.	ERC
	22.7.17		Parade for men not going into the line. Remainder prepared guns and Equipment.	
		8.30pm	At 8.30 pm. the parties marched off at an interval of 3 minutes. Reached positions allotted them without casualties.	ERC
	23.7.17		Parades. Officers & men in line withdrawn at 9.0 a.m. No casualties. A second party consisting of 2 Officers and 36 men sent into line for Instruction with the 112th M.G. Coy. Arrangements made for their rations to be cooked along with remainder of 112 M.G. Coy.	ERC
	24-7-17		Parades and baths for men back from the line. Guns, spare parts, limbers cleaned and one hours physical training. Report from line "No casualties"	ERC
	25.7.17		The Ranks in the line withdrawn - no casualties. Hot meal waiting for them on their return to Camp. Field oven built. Cook house whitewashed.	ERC

(A7092). Wt. W12839/M1293. 750,000. 1/17. D. D. & L., Ltd. Forms/C.2118/14.

Instructions regarding War Diaries and Intelligence Summaries are contained in F. S. Regs., Part II. and the Staff Manual respectively. Title pages will be prepared in manuscript.

WAR DIARY
or
INTELLIGENCE SUMMARY.
(Erase heading not required.)

Army Form C. 2118.

Place	Date	Hour	Summary of Events and Information	Remarks and references to Appendices
Camp	26.7.17		Parades - Gun cleaning. P.T.	SRC
	27.7.17		Parades do do do limber cleaning.	SRC
	28.7.17		Preparations made for two complete Sections with 12 spare men to go into the line on the 29th inst. Remainder of Company - ordinary parades. Instructions received as to probable dispositions of the Company in the coming operations.	SRC.
	29.7.17.		The two Sections and spare men warned for the line. Gun positions and targets notified and all calculations made and checked.	SRC.

Ref map. WYTSCHAETE 28 S.W2 (5A) $\frac{1}{10000}$

Gun Positions	Target -
No 1 Section	
	Bridge
I O 27 b 37.11.	O.30 a. 3.1.
II O 27 b. 23.26	O.30 a 3.1
III O.27. b. 06.64	Farm O.30.c 50.72.
IV O 27. b. 1.5	do.
No 2 Section	
I RE[illegible]AGNE FARM. O.33 b. 6.9.	LINE of TREES, through O.29. b. 7.1.

(A7092). Wt. W12839/M1293. 750,000. 1/17. D. D. & L., Ltd. Forms/C.2118/14.

Instructions regarding War Diaries and Intelligence Summaries are contained in F. S. Regs., Part II. and the Staff Manual respectively. Title pages will be prepared in manuscript.

WAR DIARY
or
INTELLIGENCE SUMMARY.
(Erase heading not required.)

Army Form C. 2118.

Place	Date	Hour	Summary of Events and Information	Remarks and references to Appendices
Camp.	29.7.17		Gun Position / Target	
			II 0.27.a.40.18. / 0.29.b.7.1.	SRC
			III + IV 0.27.a.35.25. / RAILWAY. 0.30 a 0.4.	
		8.35	At 8.35 p.m. No 1 Section moved off followed 5 minutes later by No 2 Section. The Transport under Shell fire at ULSTER DUMP suffered no harm.	
	30.7.17		Report from LINE – No casualties to men – 1 gun damaged and out of action. Another gun sent up and the damaged one returned to Coy. H.Q.	SRC
		11.50pm	Report through :- all well no casualties	
Camp.	31.7.17		The two Sections were not to fire during the 1st Phase but were to concentrate their attention on enemy aircraft.	SRC.

(A7092). Wt. W12839/M1293. 750,000. 1/17. D. D. & L., Ltd. Forms/C.2118/14.

Month ending July. 1917

SRCunliffe? Lt
OC 37th Bn M.G. Coy

I

Instructions regarding War Diaries and Intelligence Summaries are contained in F. S. Regs., Part II. and the Staff Manual respectively. Title pages will be prepared in manuscript.

WAR DIARY
~~or~~
~~INTELLIGENCE SUMMARY.~~
(Erase heading not required.)

247 M.G. Coy:
B.E.F.

Army Form C. 2118.

Place	Date	Hour	Summary of Events and Information	Remarks and references to Appendices
			Ref. 1/10,000. "WYTSCHAETE". 28. S.W. 2.	
Between MESSINES and OOSTTAVERNE	JULY. 31.		On this day the offensive E. of YPRES opened. This company had 8 guns in the line (Nos 1 & 2. Sections), between MESSINES & OOSTTAVERNE. They were situated as follows:-	
			1 Gun at DESPAGNE FARM 3 " in "Y" TRENCH, 4 " along GUN ROAD.	
		3.50 A.M. to 4.50 A.M.	Guns were mounted at dawn. During first phase (3.50 - 4.50 a.m) all guns were on anti-aircraft duty. No hostile 'planes appeared, so we did not fire at all. Guns were dismounted at 4.50 a.m.	
		7.30 A.M.	Guns were remounted at 7.30 a.m. in battle positions and laid as follows:-	
		7.50 A.M. to 9.50 A.M.	Nos 1-4 Guns on Trench running from O. 29. d. 65. 65. to O. 29. b. 70. 15.	
			5 & 6 " ARROW FARM O. 30. a. 5. 1.	
			7 & 8 " Bridge over WAMBEEK at O. 30. a. 34. 13.	
			During second phase (7.50 - 9.50 a.m) all guns fired on above targets according to secret instructions.	
			About 50,000 rounds of ammunition were expended altogether. There was no special retaliation.	
		6.0 P.M.	At 6.0 p.m Nos 1-4 Guns fired "rapid" on trench at O. 29. b. 7. 0. for 15 mins.	

(A7092). Wt. W12839/M1293. 750,000. 1/17. D. D. & L., Ltd. Forms/C.2118/14.

WAR DIARY

247 M.G. Coy

Aug 1917

Vol 2

II.

Instructions regarding War Diaries and Intelligence Summaries are contained in F. S. Regs., Part II. and the Staff Manual respectively. Title pages will be prepared in manuscript.

WAR DIARY
~~or~~
INTELLIGENCE SUMMARY.
(Erase heading not required.)

Army Form C. 2118.

Place	Date	Hour	Summary of Events and Information	Remarks and references to Appendices
Between MESSINES and OOSTTAVERNE.	July 31.		S.A.A. Supply. At night 40,000 rds were brought up and distributed among the gun teams. Another 40,000 rds were dumped at DERRY HOUSE in reserve. There were no casualties, but 99227, Pte COOPER. E. reported sick with swollen hands, and was admitted to No: 53 Field Ambulance.	
	Aug 1.	9.0 P.M. to 10.30 P.M.	In accordance with orders received from the D.M.G.O. all guns employed harassing fire on the same targets as on the previous day from 9 - 10.30 p.m. The guns fired intermittently on the same targets during night of Aug 1st/2nd. Ammunition expended to date - about 100,000 rds.	
	Aug. 2.		Gun Teams 1 - 4 suffering from wet and exposure. "Tommies' Cookers" Charcoal & Whale Oil issued. O.C. Coy: visited Bect: H.Q. in the morning. During the evening No: 99111 Pte MAC MILLAN J. was gassed and taken away to First Aid Station near DERRY HOUSE. The enemy were shelling ULSTER DUMP badly, and No: 99715, Pte GRAHAM. R. and No: 99550, Pte REID. R. were killed there while	

(A7092). Wt. W12839/M1293. 750,000. 1/17. D. D. & L., Ltd. Forms/C.2118/14.

III

Instructions regarding War Diaries and Intelligence Summaries are contained in F. S. Regs., Part II. and the Staff Manual respectively. Title pages will be prepared in manuscript.

WAR DIARY
or
INTELLIGENCE SUMMARY.
(Erase heading not required.)

Army Form C. 2118.

Place	Date	Hour	Summary of Events and Information	Remarks and references to Appendices
Between MESSINES and OOSTTAVERNE	Aug. 2.		carrying rations to Sect. HQ.	
	Aug. 3.		Harassing fire was employed on a line stretching from O. 29. b. 7. 0. to O. 23. d. 80. 55. About 56,000 rds were expended in this operation. Four men of No. 2 Section reported sick and were returned to duty. During the night No. 3 Section relieved No. 2 Section No. 99278, Pte BAILEY. J. C. was sent back to camp with sore feet. He failed to report and was missing for some days. He was eventually found at No. 1. Australian C.C.S. at BAILLEUL. He has since been sent down to the base. On this day too the number of men in the line was reduced to a minimum, only 1 N.C.O. + 4 men per gun being retained. No casualties in addition to those last mentioned.	
	Aug. 4.		Nothing to report except prolonged German shelling of Y TRENCH, GUN ROAD, and ULSTER DUMP.	
	Aug. 5.		Guns laid on special targets until 10 p.m. when they were changed to S.O.S. lines.	

(A5092) Wt. W12839/M1293. 750,000. 1/17. D. D. & L., Ltd. Forms/C.2118/14.

IV.

Instructions regarding War Diaries and Intelligence Summaries are contained in F. S. Regs., Part II. and the Staff Manual respectively. Title pages will be prepared in manuscript.

WAR DIARY

or

~~INTELLIGENCE SUMMARY.~~

(Erase heading not required.)

Army Form C. 2118.

Place	Date	Hour	Summary of Events and Information	Remarks and references to Appendices
Between MESSINES and OOSTTAVERNE	Aug. 5. (contd)		No. 4 Section entered line and relieved a section of 111 M.G. Coy. Very heavy shelling of ULSTER DUMP coincident with German counter-attack on HOLLEBEKE. Gas shells on "Y" Trench. No casualties.	
	Aug. 6.		No. 2 Sect relieved No. 1 Sect. No. 17417, Sgt. ORMISTON J., slightly wounded in the head just before relief took place. He was evacuated and is now off the strength of the coy.	
	Aug. 7.		Guns fired on special targets.	
CAMP AT N.31.d.1.2.	Aug. 8.		Nos 2, 3 & 4 Sects relieved by troops of 4th Australian Div and returned to camp.	
PALLAS FM. N.9.d.7.8.	Aug. 9.		Left camp at N.31.d.1.2. at 3.30 pm and marched to new camp at PALLAS FARM. N.9.d.7.8. Scanty accommodation. Men erected bivouacs with materials taken from disused dugouts. N.B. While in camp at N.31.d.1.2. this coy. had furnished one section for anti-aircraft work at Div: H.Q.	
	Aug. 10. & 11.		Time given up to preparing bivouacs, cleaning and arranging the camp and cleaning limbers, erecting cook houses, latrines, etc.	

(A7092). Wt. W12839/M1293. 750,000. 1/17. D. D. & L., Ltd. Forms/C.2118/14.

V.

Instructions regarding War Diaries and Intelligence Summaries are contained in F. S. Regs., Part II. and the Staff Manual respectively. Title pages will be prepared in manuscript.

WAR DIARY
or
~~INTELLIGENCE SUMMARY.~~

(Erase heading not required.)

Army Form C. 2118.

Place	Date	Hour	Summary of Events and Information	Remarks and references to Appendices
PALLAS FARM	Aug 12.	9.0 P.M.	Four guns (No. 1 Sect.) relieved a section of 63 M.G. Coy. No. 1 Sect. was under O.C. 112 M.G. Coy. while in the line. Guns situated as follows:-	
WEST of BUG WOOD.			Nos 1 & 2. E. of OOSTTAVERNE, about O.21.b.85.85 " 3 & 4. W. of BUG WOOD & Sect HQ " about O.15.d.3.6.	
			O.C. No 1 Sect. made reconnaissances of areas of ground for possible defensive positions with fields of direct fire as ordered by D.M.G.O.	
	Aug 13.		Repaired two of the gun positions and constructed one new one	
	Aug 14.		All four guns fired on special targets in conjunction with howitzers, as follows:- No 1 Gun Cross Tracks at O.18.a.8.6 " 2 " High Farm O.18.c.3.2. " 3 " Bomb " O.18.c.6.9 " 4 " Bomb " O.18.c.6.9. Ammunition expended about 4,000 rds	
	Aug 15.		Anti-aircraft and poles arrived from 112 M.G. Coy Advd H.Q. Erected A.A. poles at O.15.d.5.8 & O.21.b.90.85	

(A7092). Wt. W12839/M1293. 750,000. 1/17. D. D. & L., Ltd. Forms/C.2118/14.

VI.

Instructions regarding War Diaries and Intelligence Summaries are contained in F. S. Regs., Part II. and the Staff Manual respectively. Title pages will be prepared in manuscript.

WAR DIARY
or
~~INTELLIGENCE SUMMARY.~~

(Erase heading not required.)

Army Form C. 2118.

Place	Date	Hour	Summary of Events and Information	Remarks and references to Appendices
West of Bug Wood.	Aug. 15 (contd)		O.C 2, 3 & 4 Sects came into line to learn situation.	
			No 99211, L/Cpl. DAVIES. L. was killed by a shell in his dugout about 5 a.m on this day. His body was buried by the 8th (Service) Battn Somerset L.I at Cross Roads by JUNCTION BUILDINGS. O.17 c.6.5. No of deceased's disc is 672.	
	Aug 16	4.45 A.M. to 5.45 A.M.	All guns of No 1 Sect. fired on special targets from 4.45 – 5.45 a.m in conjunction with offensive operations to the North. Targets as follows:-	
			No. 1 Gun Cross Tracks at O.18 a.8.6.	
			2 " High Farm O.18 c.3.2	
			3 " Bomb " O.18 c.6.9.	
			4 " Bomb O.18 c.6.9	
			Guns fired again during day in conjunction with heavy howitzers. Targets as follows:-	
			No 1 Gun High Farm O.18 c.3.2.	
			2 " Cross Tracks. O.18 a.8.6.	
			3 " Farm. O.18 c.8.0	
			4 " Farm. O.18 c.8.0.	
			Ammunition expended during day about 11,000 rds	
		9.0 P.M.	At night No 2 Section relieved No 1 Section, and Nos 2 & 3 Sections relieved two sections of 112 M.G. Coy. No casualties.	

(A7092) Wt. W12839/M1293 750,000. 1/17. D. D. & L., Ltd. Forms/C.2118/14.

VII.

Instructions regarding War Diaries and Intelligence Summaries are contained in F. S. Regs., Part II. and the Staff Manual respectively. Title pages will be prepared in manuscript.

WAR DIARY
or
~~INTELLIGENCE~~ SUMMARY.

(*Erase heading not required.*)

Army Form C. 2118.

Place	Date	Hour	Summary of Events and Information	Remarks and references to Appendices
OOSTTAVERNE. WEST of BUG WOOD. ROSE WOOD.	Aug 16 (contd)		Distribution of 12 guns (Nos 2, 3 + 4 Secᵗˢ) of this coy: 4 Guns. A.1–4 E. of OOSTTAVERNE in O.21.b. 4 Guns. A.5–8. W. of BUG WOOD in O.15.d 2 Guns ROSE WOOD in O.16.a. 2 Guns B.1 & B.2. (to fire only in case of hostile attack) While in the line Nos 2, 3 + 4 Secᵗˢ were under O.C. 63 M.G. Coy.	
	Aug 17 to Aug 22.		All guns except B.1 + B.2. fired on special targets, viz woods, tracks and strong points behind German line. Guns A.1. – A.8. were laid on barrage line from O.24.a.2.4. to O.18.c.4.9. Guns did not fire on this line, as no S.O.S. signals were observed during this period. Officers, & N.C.O.s were fully occupied reconnoitring and making tracings and reports with a view to selection of defence positions with good fields of direct fire. Hostile artillery was not very active during this period in our zone. Weather remained fine, and the men after working on their dugouts, were fairly comfortable, with the exception of forward teams (B.1. + B.2.) whose dugouts remained wet.	

(A7092) Wt. W12839/M1293. 750,000. 1/17. D. D. & L., Ltd. Forms/C.2118/14.

VIII.

Instructions regarding War Diaries and Intelligence Summaries are contained in F. S. Regs., Part II. and the Staff Manual respectively. Title pages will be prepared in manuscript.

WAR DIARY

~~or~~

~~INTELLIGENCE SUMMARY.~~

(Erase heading not required.)

Army Form C. 2118.

Place	Date	Hour	Summary of Events and Information	Remarks and references to Appendices
DAMM STRASSE.	Aug. 19		Signalling Cpl. arrived at Advd Coy. H.Q. in DAMM STRASSE for course of instruction.	
			German 'plane brought down in evening.	
	Aug. 20.	9. a.m.	Another German 'plane was brought down about 9 a.m. and fell near Advd Coy. H.Q.	
			No 105,912 Pte MAC MILLAN R. has been missing since this day. He was last seen at dawn carrying rations from Sect. H.Q. at O.16.c.35.45 to Shell Hole Line.	
WEST of BUG WOOD	Aug. 22.	7.50 P.M.	No 1 Sect. relieved No 4 Sect in A.5 – A.8 positions. Nos 2 & 3 were relieved by two sections of 112 MG Coy. No 1 Sect was under O.C. 112 MG Coy. again.	
	Aug. 23.		O.C. No 1 Sect altered positions of guns A.5., A.6, & A.7, placing guns about 10x in front of former positions, which were in a new communication trench W of BUG WOOD.	
			Instructions re anti aircraft measures arrived. O.C. No 1 Sect told off one team per day as A.A. Gunners.	
			All guns fired harassing fire during the night in conjunction with howitzers on following targets:—	
			SPUD FARM. O.18.b.2.9.	
			MURPHY " O.18.b.3.7.	

(A7092). Wt. W12839/M1293. 750,000. 1/17. D. D. & L., Ltd. Forms/C.2118/14.

IX.

Instructions regarding War Diaries and Intelligence Summaries are contained in F. S. Regs., Part II. and the Staff Manual respectively. Title pages will be prepared in manuscript.

WAR DIARY

~~or~~

~~INTELLIGENCE SUMMARY.~~

(Erase heading not required.)

Army Form C. 2118.

Place	Date	Hour	Summary of Events and Information	Remarks and references to Appendices
West of Bog Wood.	Aug. 23. (contd.)		Low Fm } 0.18 c. 5.0. Centre } 0.18 c. 4.1. About 1000 rds were expended	
	Aug. 24.	1.0 A.M. - 8.0 A.M.	All guns fired on High Fm. 0.18 c 25 20 and Poll Fm 0.18 a. 75. 53. at 1 & 8 a.m. About 500 rds expended.	
	Aug. 25		All guns fired on { Centre Fm 0.18. c. 4.1. Low " 0.18 c. 5.0. Spud " 0.18. b. 2.9. About 3000 rds expended.	
	Aug. 26.		Practice S.O.S. went up. Guns fired on S.O.S. lines, 0.18. c.4.9. to 0.18 c. 35. 05. All guns fired on following targets during afternoon in conjunction with artillery. { Murphy Fm. 0.18. b. 3.7 Dugouts at 0.18.b. 45. 30. Tracks " 0.18 central Tracks. 0.18 b 0.5. About 5,500 rds expended	
	Aug. 27.	2.32 A.M. to 3.0 A.M.	To cover raid on BEE Fm all guns opened fire at 2.32 a.m on following targets:–	

(A7092). Wt. W12839/M1293. 750,000. 1/17. D. D. & L., Ltd. Forms/C.2118/14.

F

WAR DIARY

~~or~~

~~INTELLIGENCE SUMMARY.~~

(Erase heading not required.)

Army Form C. 2118.

Instructions regarding War Diaries and Intelligence Summaries are contained in F. S. Regs., Part II. and the Staff Manual respectively. Title pages will be prepared in manuscript.

Place	Date	Hour	Summary of Events and Information	Remarks and references to Appendices
West of Bog Wood.	Aug 27 (contd)		FLY BUILDINGS 0. 23. b. 62. 76.	
			LOW F^M R^D 0. 18. c. 55. 02.	
			CENTRE " 0. 18. c 4. 1.	
			HIGH " 0. 18. c. 25. 20.	
			Guns fired till 3 a.m when "All in" signal went. There was no retaliation in our zone.	
			All guns fired on POLL F^M 0.18 a 75. in the afternoon.	
			Guns fired during night on tracks in 0. 18 central (and " at 0. 18. b. 0. 5.	
			Ammunition expended - about 7000 rds (whole day).	
	Aug 28	7.45 P.M.	No 1 Sect relieved by No 4 Sect at 7.45pm in A.5 - A.8 positions. No 4 Sect under OC 111 M.G. Coy while in the line	
	Aug 29		O.C. No 4 Sect carried out reconnaissance of new positions.	
	Aug 30		2/Lieuts GLANVILLE & EDWARDS become attached to Rifle B^de in the line for tour of instruction with infantry.	
	Aug 31		No 3 Sect went up to line to 63 M.G. Coy to take up positions for barrage fire.	
			During all this period the sections that remained in camp spent their ~~time~~ in training viz: P.T., Route Marches, Gun Work. etc - and in cleaning limbers.	
			E. G. Cruickshank. 247 Coy, M.G.C.	

(A7092). Wt. W12839/M1293. 750,000. 1/17. D. D. & L., Ltd. Forms/C.2118/14.

Vol 3

War Diary

247th M.G. Coy

Sept 1917

Instructions regarding War Diaries and Intelligence Summaries are contained in F. S. Regs., Part II. and the Staff Manual respectively. Title pages will be prepared in manuscript.

WAR DIARY
or
INTELLIGENCE SUMMARY.
(Erase heading not required.)

Army Form C. 2118.

Place	Date	Hour	Summary of Events and Information	Remarks and references to Appendices
PALAIS FARM.	1-9-17		In Camp - Gun Drill - Physical Training - Lectures.	
			No 3 Section in line - WHITE CHATEAU WOOD - relieved one Section of 228 M.G. Coy.	
			No 4 Section - " - PRESTON DUMP under orders of O.C. 111 M.G. Coy. No casualties	
			Fired on S.O.S. lines and harassing fire.	
PALAIS FARM.	2.9.17.		No 2 Section in Camp - General routine work.	
			No 1 Section take up position in the line WEST of BATTLE WOOD.	
			No 3 Section in line - WHITE CHATEAU WOOD - This Section was withdrawn at dusk.	
			No 4 Section in line - near PRESTON DUMP.	
PALAIS FARM.	3-9-17		Nos 1 and 3 Sections relieved No 228 M.G. Coy, 39th Division in positions WEST of BATTLE WOOD.	
			No 2 Section with 2 guns of No 3 Section took over "C" Battery of 6 guns.	
			No 1 Section with 2 guns of No 3 Section took over "D" Battery of 6 guns.	
			The Guns were laid on their respective S.O.S. lines.	
			2Lt EDWARDS and 2Lt GLANVILLE were attached to the 13th Bn K.R.R. for instruction with INFANTRY in occupation of the shell-hole line.	
LINE	4.9.17		O.C. Nos 1, 2, + 3 Sections made a reconnaissance of the ground in front and to the flanks of their positions. There was no firing by day but intermittent harassing fire throughout the night.	

(A7092). Wt. W12839/M1293. 750,000. 1/17. D. D. & L., Ltd. Forms/C.2118/14.

Instructions regarding War Diaries and Intelligence Summaries are contained in F. S. Regs., Part II. and the Staff Manual respectively. Title pages will be prepared in manuscript.

WAR DIARY
or
INTELLIGENCE SUMMARY.
(Erase heading not required.)

Army Form C. 2118.

Place	Date	Hour	Summary of Events and Information	Remarks and references to Appendices
LINE.	5.9.17.		Slight GAS SHELL attack about 4.30 a.m. Nothing serious and no casualties. A hostile aeroplane was brought down by our aircraft near FUSILIER WOOD about 9.0 a.m. O^s C Nos 1,2,+3 Sections again made a reconnaissance of the ground in front of their respective positions. Harassing fire was again carried out throughout the night.	
	6.9.17.		Officers of No 246 Machine Gun Company came to reconnoitre positions for guns for the coming attack. 19th Division.	
	7.9.17		Reconnaissance by O^s C. 1,2+3 Sections. Fired on S.O.S. lines about 7.30 p.m. Prompt retaliation by German Artillery using 77 m.m shells. No damage - no casualties.	
	8.9.17		Reconnaissance by Section Commanders and the usual harassing fire. No incident to report.	
	9.9.17		OC. No 4 Section went to the line to reconnoitre for positions near HOLLEBEKE for our guns during the impending attack. S.O.S. signal was observed at 7.30 p.m. and the guns immediately opened fire on the S.O.S. line.	
	10.9.17		Slight German shelling of our positions about 4.0 p.m. No material damage or casualties	
	11.9.17		Gas shell attacks on our positions at about 1.0 a.m. 3 a.m. and 4.30 a.m. Box respirators put on - No casualties.	

(A7092). Wt. W12839/M1293. 750,000. 1/17. D. D. & L., Ltd. Forms/C.2118/14.

Army Form C. 2118.

Instructions regarding War Diaries and Intelligence Summaries are contained in F. S. Regs., Part II. and the Staff Manual respectively. Title pages will be prepared in manuscript.

WAR DIARY
or
INTELLIGENCE SUMMARY.

(Erase heading not required.)

Place	Date	Hour	Summary of Events and Information.	Remarks and references to Appendices
LINE. W. of BATTLE WOOD	11-9-17		One of our 'planes was brought down by a howitzer shell striking it. The aeroplane fell in our lines. An Ammunition Dump near HILL 60 was hit and blown up by hostile artillery fire about 7.30 p.m.	
	12.9.17		O.C. Coy. and O^C. Sections made a reconnaissance of the ground NORTH of HOLLEBEKE about 5.30 a.m. No incident to report. Normal artillery fire.	
	13-9-17		Nos 1 2 + 3 Sections were withdrawn at 4.30 a.m. and returned to Transport Lines at PALAIS FARM. Remainder of day devoted to cleaning impedimenta, Equipment and baths.	
PALAIS FARM	14-9-17		During the day only Physical Training and Close Order Drill were carried out.	
		5.0 pm	At 5.0 p.m. all Officers - N.C.O.s and available men went up to the line and commenced work on positions previously selected NORTH of HOLLEBEKE. Work was carried on throughout the hours of darkness and at daybreak the whole party returned to the Transport Lines.	
	15.9.17.		The procedure of the previous day was repeated, the new positions being completed and camouflaged. 320,000 S.A.A. were taken up to the line and 20000 rounds per gun were placed in the shelters constructed for belt filling. At dawn the party returned to the Transport Lines with the exception of sentries left behind to guard the S.A.A.	
	16.9.17. 17.9.17. 18.9.17.		The time was devoted to rehearsing our part in the coming attack - to tuning up the guns and to thoroughly examining all parts, belts etc. Maps showing exactly the task of Each Battery were made and handed over to Section Officers.	

(A7092). Wt. W12839/M1293. 750,000. 1/17. D. D. & L., Ltd. Forms/C.2118/14.

Instructions regarding War Diaries and Intelligence Summaries are contained in F. S. Regs., Part II. and the Staff Manual respectively. Title pages will be prepared in manuscript.

WAR DIARY
or
INTELLIGENCE SUMMARY.
(Erase heading not required.)

Army Form C. 2118.

Place	Date	Hour	Summary of Events and Information	Remarks and references to Appendices
LINE.	18.9.17		O^s C. Sections, and Nos 1 of Guns occupy new positions in the line. The remainder of the company + carrying party ~~[illegible]~~ place all guns, belts and belt boxes, spare parts, oil, etc in order to march in lightly the following night. At OAK DUMP an Artillery barrage opened at 8.30 pm Two men of No 4 Section – Ptes MONCAR and READ were slightly wounded, and one mule killed by one of our own shells which exploded prematurely	
	19.9.17		O.C. Coy. and the remainder of the Coy. moved off from the Transport lines to take up their positions in the line. At Dusk O^s C. Sections laid guns on ZERO LINES – One Aiming Stick put out in the correct position to represent the ZERO LINE. Luminous paint was painted on to the aiming sticks but the luminosity obtained was found to be unsatisfactory - only a slight glow being obtained after having applied several coats of paint. The Sections dispositions were as follows. No 1 Section – D1 BATTERY No 2 Section – E2 BATTERY No 3 Section – C BATTERY No 4 Section – D11 BATTERY. – Opportunity Guns. 40 Metal Belts were used during the period but were thought to be unsatisfactory.	

(A7092). Wt. W12839/M1293. 750,000. 1/17. D. D. & L., Ltd. Forms/C.2118/14.

Instructions regarding War Diaries and Intelligence Summaries are contained in F. S. Regs., Part II. and the Staff Manual respectively. Title pages will be prepared in manuscript.

WAR DIARY
or
INTELLIGENCE SUMMARY.
(Erase heading not required.)

Army Form C. 2118.

Place	Date	Hour	Summary of Events and Information	Remarks and references to Appendices
LINE	20.9.17		Opened fire at ZERO HOUR (5.40 a.m.) and fired at the following rates:- I 60 rounds per minute till 8.10 a.m. II 25 – – – – 9.40 a.m. III 50 – – – – 11.10 a.m. IV 25 – – – – 3.0 p.m. "CEASE FIRE" was then communicated by the D.M.G.O. There was slight GERMAN retaliation on our positions whilst D2 BATTERY received great attention from hostile artillery. Telephonic communication between the BATTERIES and the D.M.G.O. at DELBSKE FARM was destroyed the wire being cut by the enemy shell fire. S.O.S. went up on our left at 7.30 p.m. Fire was opened and was continued until the situation became clear. About 8.0 p.m. 2000 rounds per gun were expended. The retaliation on D1, C, and E BATTERIES was only moderate but D2 BATTERY was heavily shelled. Casualties:- 2/LIEUT MARSHALL, O.C. D2 BATTERY was evacuated, suffering from shell shock. L CPL COOK, L CPL PATERSON received slight wounds and were returned to the Transport Lines.	

(A7092). Wt. W12839/M1293. 750,000. 1/17. D. D. & L., Ltd. Forms/C.2118/14.

Instructions regarding War Diaries and Intelligence Summaries are contained in F. S. Regs., Part II. and the Staff Manual respectively. Title pages will be prepared in manuscript.

WAR DIARY
or
INTELLIGENCE SUMMARY.
(Erase heading not required.)

Army Form C. 2118.

Place	Date	Hour	Summary of Events and Information	Remarks and references to Appendices
LINE	20.9.17		CPL CROPPER, PTES PLATT and HUSSEY were wounded slightly, inoculated and sent to the Transport Lines. PTES GLEN and WOODALL were wounded and admitted to HOSPITAL	
	21.9.17		We opened fire at 4.30 a.m. because the artillery bombardment began but no S.O.S. had been observed.	
			S.O.S. was sent up at 7.0 p.m. We opened fire immediately and continued to fire until 8.0 p.m. when everything became normal. 2000 rounds per gun were expended. One of our BALLOONS was brought down in flames by an Enemy aeroplane. Harassing fire was employed during the night on selected targets.	
LINE	22.9.17		About 8.0 a.m. a British 'Plane (BRISTOL SCOUT) was brought down by hostile anti-aircraft fire and fell in OAK AVENUE, about 200x WEST of D1 BATTERY. The Enemy shelled the place for a short time.	
			From 12 noon to 12.45 p.m. Enemy shelled the region of D1 and D2 BATTERIES and SUPPORT LINE fairly heavily. No casualties and no damage to positions.	
			German ALBATROSS SCOUTS flying low over our front line nearly every half hour warned men of D1 and D2 BATTERIES to keep especially low	
			Henceforward guns on S.O.S. lines all the time and no firing done except in case of S.O.S.	

(A7092). Wt. W12839/M1293. 750,000. 1/17. D. D. & L., Ltd. Forms/C.2118/14.

Instructions regarding War Diaries and Intelligence Summaries are contained in F. S. Regs., Part II. and the Staff Manual respectively. Title pages will be prepared in manuscript.

WAR DIARY
or
INTELLIGENCE SUMMARY.
(Erase heading not required.)

Army Form C. 2118.

Place	Date	Hour	Summary of Events and Information	Remarks and references to Appendices
LINE.	23.9.17		Increased hostile aerial activity. Enemy 'planes trying to cross our first line at a low altitude nearly every half hour. They were engaged by Anti aircraft guns and by Machine Guns and did not penetrate the support line.	
			About 6.0 p.m. a hostile 'plane ALBATROSS SCOUT was brought down by one of our TRIPLANES.	
	24.9.17		C, D1, D2 + E Batteries withdrew from the line under orders of the D.M.G.O. and returned to the Transport lines.	
			As our last Section (D1) was passing OAK DUMP our Artillery opened a barrage. There was no immediate retaliation and no casualties.	
			The S.A.A. remaining (about 30000 rounds) was handed over to O.C. MANCHESTER REGT. at BOW. H.Q.	
PALAIS FARM	25.9.17		Whole of 247 M.G. Coy. left PALAIS FARM at 1.30 p.m. and marched via SCHERPENBERG and WESTOUTRE to billets in a farm at MT KOKEREELE and BERTHEN.	
			Arrived in billets about 5.0 p.m.	
	26.9.17		Orders to have belts filled and ourselves ready to move at very short notice received. Everyone confined to Camp pending further orders or information	
			Guns cleaned and lined up in readiness. Inspected by the O.C. Company.	

(A7092). Wt. W12839/M1293. 750,000. 1/17. D. D. & L., Ltd. Forms/C.2118/14.

Instructions regarding War Diaries and Intelligence Summaries are contained in F. S. Regs., Part II. and the Staff Manual respectively. Title pages will be prepared in manuscript.

WAR DIARY
or
INTELLIGENCE SUMMARY.
(Erase heading not required.)

Army Form C. 2118.

Place	Date	Hour	Summary of Events and Information	Remarks and references to Appendices
BERTHEN	27.9.17		Gun work and dial reading practised.	
			About 3.30 pm orders for move received and preparations were made forthwith. All available stores were packed whilst all the necessary gun material was packed in two limbers - one half limber per section.	
BERTHEN	28.9.17		MOTOR BUSSES arrived at 8.30 a.m. to convey the Company to the line. Arrangements were made with O°C 117 and 228 M.G. Coys. for the taking over of tripods and belts and belt boxes. This was carried out.	
			The Company was debussed at BOS HOUSE where guides from 117 and 228 M.G. Coys. were to meet us. The relief was carried out without a hitch.	
			Notice was received this early morning that the Transport lines was to be moved the following morning.	
LINE	29.9.17		Transport lines moved in accordance with instructions received to WILLEBEKE CAMP.	
			Normal activity in the line.	

E.L. Cunliffe Lieut.
247 M.G. Coy.
2-10-17.

(A7092). Wt. W12839/M1293. 750,000. 1/17. D. D. & L., Ltd. Forms/C.2118/14.

War Diary

247 M G Coy

Oct 1917.

Army Form C. 2118.

Instructions regarding War Diaries and Intelligence Summaries are contained in F. S. Regs., Part II. and the Staff Manual respectively. Title pages will be prepared in manuscript.

WAR DIARY
or
INTELLIGENCE SUMMARY.
(Erase heading not required.)

Place	Date	Hour	Summary of Events and Information	Remarks and references to Appendices
Line.	Oct. 1.		The whole Company in the line, attached to the 111th Infantry Brigade.	Ref Map 1/10000 SHREWSBURY FOREST AREA.
			Company Headquarters in the Tunnels at J 30. b. 3 8.	
			The disposition of the Company as follows :-	
			No. 1 and 2 Sections with 8 guns formed "F" Battery and were situated in CLONMEL COPSE J 19. c. 4. 4.	
			No. 3 and 4 Sections with 8 Guns — "D" Battery - - - - J. 25 a. 40. 62.	
			No firing was done during the day. At 4.0 p.m. an enemy aeroplane was observed to come down in the direction of SANCTUARY WOOD.	
			At 7.15 p.m. S.O.S. was observed to go up on the front of the Division on our left. We opened fire for safety and continued to fire till 7.55 p.m. when the situation appeared to be normal.	
			Ammunition expended D Battery : 17000 / F do : 15000 } = 32,000 rounds.	
			The Enemy retaliated by shelling our area with heavy shells from 10.5 p.m. to 10.45 p.m. and intermittently throughout the night.	
			No casualties were caused and no damage to our positions.	
Line.	Oct. 2.		A new Officer, 2Lieut REEVES. F came up the line for duty and was posted to No 4 Section, D Battery. He replaced Lieut MARSHALL who was evacuated - sick - on the 20-9-17. Enemy shelled our area heavily from 6.15 p.m. – 7.45 p.m.	

D. D. & L., London, E.C.
(A8001) Wt. W1771/M2031 750,000 5/17 Sch. 52 Forms/C2118/14

Instructions regarding War Diaries and Intelligence Summaries are contained in F. S. Regs., Part II. and the Staff Manual respectively. Title pages will be prepared in manuscript.

WAR DIARY
or
INTELLIGENCE SUMMARY.
(Erase heading not required.)

Army Form C. 2118.

Place	Date	Hour	Summary of Events and Information	Remarks and references to Appendices
Line.	OCT. 2.	–	and intermittently throughout the night.	
	OCT. 3.		Preparations were made for the next days firing. At 4.15 p.m. S.O.S. was observed to go up some distance to the NORTH. D Battery opened fire and 14000 rounds were expended.	
			CASUALTIES. 99722 Pte BEREN. H.T. slightly wounded.	
			99548 Pte LOFTUS. G. Shell shock	
			99187 Pte SKINNER. F.J. do To TRANSPORT LINES, since evacuated.	
LINE.	OCT 4.		ACTIVE OPERATIONS.	
		6.0 am	All guns opened fire at ZERO HOUR (6.0 a.m.) and fired at a slow rate till 9.0 a.m. TARGETS. D BATTERY. J. 27 b. 02.00 – J 27 c. 45. 25.	
			F. BATTERY J 27. b. 55.75. – J 27 b. 02. 00.	
			4 guns of each battery fired on the S.O.S Targets as above, and 4 guns searched from S.O.S. lines through 2°30' of deviation.	
			Ammunition expended = 88,000 rounds.	
			There was no special retaliation.	
		6.50 pm.	S.O.S. was observed in our Sector and to the NORTH. Rapid fire was opened and was maintained for 1/4 hour. The enemy shelled our area heavily during the night and 2 guns of F Battery were put out of action.	

D. D. & L., London, E.C.
(A8001) Wt. W1771/M2031 750,000 5/17 Sch. 52 Forms/C2118/14

Instructions regarding War Diaries and Intelligence Summaries are contained in F. S. Regs., Part II. and the Staff Manual respectively. Title pages will be prepared in manuscript.

WAR DIARY
or
INTELLIGENCE SUMMARY.
(Erase heading not required.)

Army Form C. 2118.

Place	Date	Hour	Summary of Events and Information	Remarks and references to Appendices
Line.	OCT 4.		CASUALTIES. 99710 Pte CREERAR. D No 4 SECTION, D BATTERY. WOUNDED.	
			5089 BENNETT. W do do do.	
	OCT. 5	6.55pm	S.O.S. observed in our Sector at 6.55 p.m.	
			Fire was opened immediately. Ammunition expended 30000 rounds.	
			No further incident.	
	OCT. 6.		On the night Oct. 6th 7th harassing fire was carried out at 300x beyond S.O.S. lines.	
			No incident of importance	
	OCT 7 + 8		Harassing fire - Situation normal.	
	OCT 9.		All guns opened fire at 5.20 a.m. (in conjunction with offensive operations in front and to the NORTH) and fired till 6.0 a.m. at the rate of one belt per four minutes. From 6.0 a.m - 7.20 a.m. fire was maintained at the rate of one belt per 20 minutes. No special retaliation and no damage to positions.	
			The Targets were as follows:-	
			D Battery, 8 guns — J27.b.02.00 — J27c.45.25.	
			F do do — J27.b.55.75 — J.27.b.02.00.	
			4 guns of each battery fired on S.O.S. lines and 4 guns searched from	

D. D. & L., London, E.C.
(A8001) Wt. W1771/M2031 750,000 5/17 Sch. 52 Forms/C2118/14

Instructions regarding War Diaries and Intelligence Summaries are contained in F. S. Regs., Part II. and the Staff Manual respectively. Title pages will be prepared in manuscript.

WAR DIARY
or
INTELLIGENCE SUMMARY.
(Erase heading not required.)

Army Form C. 2118.

Place	Date	Hour	Summary of Events and Information	Remarks and references to Appendices
LINE.	OCT. 9	-	S.O.S lines to 2° 30' of elevation.	
			Ammunition expended during the day = 75000 rounds.	
			The enemy retaliated with very heavy shelling during the night.	
	OCT 10.	-	Two men were killed by shell fire during the early morning.	
			106874 Pte POULTON. W.J. No 1 Section F BATTERY.	
			99125 . ROBB. G. No 2 Section do.	
			These men were buried about 40x from Section H.Q. in CLONMEL COPSE. at J. 19. c. 45. 25. at 7.45 a.m.	
			The Enemy shelled our area intermittently between 6.0 p.m + 7.30 pm but the night was very quiet.	
LINE.	OCT. 11		The whole Company was relieved by the 111 M.G. Coy. at 4.0 pm met by Motor bus at SPOIL BANK and conveyed to CONFUSION CORNER.	
			The total amount of ammunition expended during the tour = 235,000	
TRANSPORT LINES.	OCT 12		Time was spent in Baths, Cleaning gun materials equipment etc.	
	OCT. 13.		Inspection by CAPT. V.A. TYLOR. Prepared for a move on the day following Orders were subsequently Cancelled.	

D. D. & L., London, E.C.
(A8001) Wt. W1771/M2031 750,000 5/17 Sch. 52 Forms/C2118/14

Instructions regarding War Diaries and Intelligence Summaries are contained in F. S. Regs., Part II. and the Staff Manual respectively. Title pages will be prepared in manuscript.

WAR DIARY
or
INTELLIGENCE SUMMARY.
(Erase heading not required.)

Army Form C. 2118.

Place	Date	Hour	Summary of Events and Information	Remarks and references to Appendices
TRANSPORT LINES.	OCT. 14		Physical Training – Route marching.	
N15 b. 4.9.	OCT. 15.		Packing limbers for move on the following day. Deficiencies. Equipment etc handed in. Exchange of clothing.	
R22 b. 7.5.	OCT. 16		The Company moved from N15 b. 4.9. to billets in the backward area arriving there about 4.30 p.m.	
R22 b 7.5	OCT. 17. OCT. 31		The time was spent in Technical Training during the mornings as per programme and the afternoons were devoted to Range work. Football, Sports, Tug of war etc.	
	OCT. 23		2/LIEUT. BURKE. was posted to the Company and was attached to No 4 Section for duty.	
	OCT 31		COY. SPORTS – PROGRAMME ATTACHED.	

E. Cunliffe Lieut.
247 M. G. Coy.

D. D. & L., London, E.C.
(A8001) Wt. W1771/M2031 750,000 5/17 Sch. 52 Forms/C2118/14

247 M. G. Co.

Training Programme for first Phase of 9 days

1st day 17.10.17	Physical Training, - Elementary Gun Drill - Squad Drill; Mechanism; Gas Drill.	
2ND " 18.10.17	P.T. - Immediate Action - Explanation of Dials - Sight Setting & Laying - Practise Route March	Signallers and R. Finders, Class
3RD " 19.10.17	P.T. - Limber Packing - Pack Saddlery - Squad & Saluting Drill - Limber Drill -	N.C.Os Class, Map Reading Signlrs & R. Finders Class Officers, Horse Mangt
4TH " 20.10.17	P.T. - Visual Training - Gun Drill - Mechanism - Lecture on discipline	N.C.O. Class, Fire direction theory Signlrs & R. Finders Class Officers - Harness
5TH " 22.10.17	Section Route March including simple Tactical exercise with guns & limbers	Officers Specialists } WITH SECTIONS N.C.Os
6TH " 23.10.17	P.T. - Fire direction - Tests of Elementary training - Lecture on indirect Fire.	Officers - Limber Inventory N.C.O's Fire direction Practice
7TH " 24.10.17	P.T. - Immediate Action - Mechanism - Range if obtainable.	Range.
8TH " 25.10.17	P.T. Lecture on Barrage fire - Practice taking up Positions & bounding	With Sections
9TH " 26.10.17	P.T. - Fire direction - Barrage Practice.	Officers Animal Mangmt.

247 M.G.C^o

* Programme of Training *

Monday Oct 29	P.T. Squad Drill & Musketry - Gun Drill - I.A. Mechanism - Range, Sports & Football	Officers Class N.C.Os " Specialists "
Tues: " 30	Tactical Scheme - Visual Training ———— Range. Sports & Football	———
Wed: 31	P.T. Indication & Recognition - Use of A.A. sights - Gun Drill ——— C^oy Sports	Officers Class N.C.Os " Specialists "
Thurs: Nov. 1	P.T. Fire Direction - Squad Drill. Rifle Exercises - I.A & Mechanism - Range & Football	.... D^o ....
Fri. " 2	P.T. - Gas Drill - Action from Limbers - Laying & Sight Setting ——— Range & Football	.... D^o ....
Sat. " 3	P.T. Pack Saddlery - Squad Drill - T.O.E.T. ——— Route March ———	.... D^o ....
Sun: " 4	P.T. Tactical Scheme. Advanced Drill ———— Range - Football	.... D^o ....
Mon: " 5	P.T. Gun Drill - Fire Direction - Limber Drill ——— Range - Football ———	.... D^o ....
Tues: 6	P.T. Indication & Recognition - Squad Drill — I.A. — Range - Football	.... D^o ....

Company Sports

EVENTS

	Points 1st	2nd	3rd
Officers 100^x flat	4.	3.	2
Sergeants 100^x flat	4.	3.	2
Corporals & men 100^x (Final)	4.	3.	2
Blindfold Squad Drill (8 per Sec)	8.	4.	—
High Jump.	4.	3.	2
440^x flat (Final)	4.	3.	2
Pillow Fight.	2.	1.	—
Tug of War. Officers & Sergeants	—	—	—
Kicking the Football (1 man per Sec)	2.	1.	—
Throwing the Hammer (Final)	2.	1.	—
½ mile flat.	4.	3.	2
Band Race.	—	—	—
Boat Race (7 per Sec 100^x with turn)	8.	4	—
Challenge Race 440^x open for entry on day	—	—	—
Wheelbarrow Race 50^x	2.	1.	—
Blindfold Driving 100^x	2.	1	—
Inter Section Relay Race 100^x 440^x 880^x	12	9.	
4 legged race. 100^x	4.	2.	—
Wrestling on Mules. (Scrum open to Secs)	4.	2.	—
Pick-a-back wrestling (Scrum)	4.	2.	—
Eating the bun.	1.	—	—
¼ mile walking	4.	3.	2
Tug of War (Final) Teams of 10.	10.	5.	—

NOV 17

247 M G Coy

Army Form C. 2118.

Vol 5

WAR DIARY
or
INTELLIGENCE SUMMARY.

(Erase heading not required.)

Instructions regarding War Diaries and Intelligence Summaries are contained in F. S. Regs., Part II. and the Staff Manual respectively. Title pages will be prepared in manuscript.

Place	Date	Hour	Summary of Events and Information	Remarks and references to Appendices
MT KOKEREEL R22b 70.50.	1st to 8th		Training was carried on according to programme whilst the afternoons were devoted to competitions in sports, football, rifle firing, boxing etc. All fwd material etc was completed and transport thoroughly overhauled. On the 6th inst. a Divisional Competition was held in connection with the YUKON PACK. Teams from the various Units of the Division were entered – each team comprising One NCO., and 10 men. The Company was fifth on the final result but an unfortunate occurrence – one man fast in barbed wire robbed us of the second place. The O.C. Company went to visit the line with the DMGO in order to reconnoitre the line before taking over. On the 7th inst the O.C. Coy went into the line and the Coy was to relieve the 246th Coy. the day following. A Divisional Transport Show took place on the 7th inst. – the Competition consisting of 1 section transport complete – including the Section Officer's Charger. The Company was second in the final judgement.	

D. D. & L., London, E.C.
(A8001) Wt. W1771/M2031 750,000 5/17 Sch. 52 Forms/C2118/14

Army Form C. 2118.

Instructions regarding War Diaries and Intelligence Summaries are contained in F. S. Regs., Part II. and the Staff Manual respectively. Title pages will be prepared in manuscript.

WAR DIARY
or
INTELLIGENCE SUMMARY.
(Erase heading not required.)

Place	Date	Hour	Summary of Events and Information	Remarks and references to Appendices
LINE.	8.11.17		The Coy. was moved from R22b.7.5 to SPOIL BANK by bus whilst the Transport moved independently to BUTTERFLY FARM. On arrival at the Transport lines it was found that 246th. M.G.Coy. was still in possession but that they were moving the morning following. Accomodation was arranged temporarily but satisfactorily. The relief of the 246th. M.G. Coy. was carried out without a hitch. On account of the move and limited accomodation rations were late in reaching their respective points – Coy. H.Q. SPOIL BANK Nos 2, 3 + 4 Sections – TRANSPORT CORNER – No 1 Section – PHEASANT DUMP. During the hours of darkness, harassing fire was maintained on Enemy tracks, dugouts, centres of movement etc. 7000 rounds were expended.	
	9.11.17		The Camp at BUTTERFLY FARM was taken over from 246th. M.G. Coy and the whole accomodation rearranged. 6000 rounds of Ammunition were fired beyond the S.O.S. lines	

D. D. & L., London, E.C.
(A8001) Wt. W1771/M2031 750,000 5/17 Sch. 52 Forms/C2118/14

Instructions regarding War Diaries and Intelligence Summaries are contained in F. S. Regs., Part II. and the Staff Manual respectively. Title pages will be prepared in manuscript.

WAR DIARY
or
INTELLIGENCE SUMMARY.
(Erase heading not required.)

Army Form C. 2118.

Place	Date	Hour	Summary of Events and Information	Remarks and references to Appendices
LINE.	9-11-17		In the early morning several low flying enemy aircraft were observed over our emplacements. Cover was made for belt boxes and new latrines commenced. Heavy hostile shelling in the region of DELBSKE FARM. 3 hostile aircraft were brought down – one at BDN. H.Q. – one Nr HOLLEBEKE and one in the Enemy's line about 10.0 a.m.	
	10-11-17		Harassing fire was carried out during the night behind the SOS lines and 4,500 rounds of ammunition were expended. Our forward gun positions were bombarded by hostile trench mortars. Hostile artillery was very active during the night in the vicinity of the gun positions and dugouts. There was no damage to emplacements, and no casualties were sustained. At 3.30 pm a hostile aeroplane was driven down out of control behind the Enemy lines.	
	11-11-17		Improvements to gun positions – dugouts etc made. Hostile artillery was quiet in the vicinity of the guns. Harassing fire was maintained on centres of enemy movement and 6000 rounds S.A.A. were expended – no casualties.	
	12-11-17		Two Sections were relieved by two sections of 112th M.G. Coy + 63rd M.G. Coy and returned to Transport lines at BUTTERFLY FARM arriving there about 11.30 pm.	

D. D. & L., London, E.C.
(A8001) Wt. W1771/M2031 750,000 5/17 Sch. 52 Forms C2118/14

Army Form C. 2118.

Instructions regarding War Diaries and Intelligence Summaries are contained in F. S. Regs., Part II. and the Staff Manual respectively. Title pages will be prepared in manuscript.

WAR DIARY
or
INTELLIGENCE SUMMARY.

(*Erase heading not required.*)

Place	Date	Hour	Summary of Events and Information	Remarks and references to Appendices
LINE.	12.11.17		Whale Oil was applied to the feet of the men on their arrival at Transport lines. The men were supplied with a hot meal	
	13.11.17		Hostile artillery was not so active as usual during the period under review but at intervals he shelled the vicinity of our gun positions and swept CHATEAU WOOD with Machine Gun fire. He caused no no casualties and no damage to our gun positions.	
			A hostile aeroplane flying low over FUSILIER WOOD fired on troops standing outside a dug out, - causing no casualties.	
			A duck board track was laid near IMPERIAL DUGOUTS and running past the gun positions.	
			2500 rounds of S.A.A were fired on tracks used by the Enemy in P.7.C.	
	14.11.17		Hostile Artillery was active in the morning in CHATEAU WOOD and round the gun positions. Hostile Aircraft was very active during the day over FUSILIER WOOD and CHATEAU WOOD. They reconnoitred the woods which were intermittently shelled. A Salvage Dump was made in FUSILIER WOOD. Range Cards, Panorama Sketches, Visual maps etc were made for the Gun positions.	
			During the night harassing fire was maintained on Enemy tracks etc - 3000 rounds S.A.A being expended.	

D. D. & L., London, E.C.
(A8001) Wt. W1771/M2031 750,000 5/17 Sch. 52 Forms/C2118/14

Army Form C. 2118.

Instructions regarding War Diaries and Intelligence Summaries are contained in F. S. Regs., Part II. and the Staff Manual respectively. Title pages will be prepared in manuscript.

WAR DIARY
or
INTELLIGENCE SUMMARY.
(Erase heading not required.)

Place	Date	Hour	Summary of Events and Information	Remarks and references to Appendices
LINE.	15.11.17		Hostile Artillery was very active day and night - the gun positions in CHATEAU WOOD, FUSILIER WOOD and the RAILWAY EMBANKMENT receiving special attention. No damage was caused to our positions.	
			Hostile aircraft was inactive.	
			Emplacements were covered in and much salving was done in the vicinity of the RAVINE.	
			3500 rounds were expended in harassing enemy tracks.	
	16.11.17		The Enemy brought Trench Mortars to bear on our forward positions - and his artillery carried out intermittent shelling of the areas in the vicinity of our positions - no casualties - no damage.	
			An Enemy Machine Gun brought fire to bear against one of our aeroplanes - doing no apparent damage.	
			One large hostile aeroplane, accompanied by six smaller craft came over our lines and directed artillery fire on our back areas.	
			Alternative emplacements commenced.	
			3000 rounds of SAA were fired on occupied dugouts - Pya 52.85.	

D. D. & L., London, E.C.
(A8001) Wt. W1771/M2031 750,000 5/17 Sch. 52 Forms/C2118/14

Instructions regarding War Diaries and Intelligence Summaries are contained in F. S. Regs., Part II. and the Staff Manual respectively. Title pages will be prepared in manuscript.

WAR DIARY
or
INTELLIGENCE SUMMARY.
(Erase heading not required.)

Army Form C. 2118.

Place	Date	Hour	Summary of Events and Information	Remarks and references to Appendices
LINE	17.11.17		Hostile Artillery was below normal activity – casual shelling – no damage – no casualties.	
			A new spare emplacement was made on the top of a dug out for direct fire down the Railway Embankment. Number Boards placed at each gun position	
			Enemy aircraft were very quiet.	
			3000 rounds S.A.A. expended during the night on Strong points near CHATEAU FARM and road running N + S. in P.8.a.	
LINE	18.11.17		Hostile Artillery more active than usual. Gas shells fell in Fusilier Wood.	
			Enemy Machine Gun was firing across OAK AVENUE	
			One Enemy Observation balloon was observed.	
			1000 rounds S.A.A were fired into BASSEVILLE WOOD.	
	19.11.17		Hostile Artillery very quiet and there was no aerial activity.	
			2000 rounds were fired on dugouts and tracks in P.1.c.	
	20.11.17		Enemy Artillery more active than usual. SPOIL BANK + CANAL WALK, CHATEAU WOOD. received his special attention.	
			Visibility was not good and his aerial activity was nil.	
			5000 rounds were fired on Centres of Enemy movement – occupied dugouts etc.	

D. D. & L., London, E.C.
(A8001) Wt. W1771/M2031 750,000 5/17 Sch. 52 Forms/C2118/14

Instructions regarding War Diaries and Intelligence Summaries are contained in F. S. Regs., Part II. and the Staff Manual respectively. Title pages will be prepared in manuscript.

WAR DIARY
or
INTELLIGENCE SUMMARY.
(Erase heading not required.)

Army Form C. 2118.

Place	Date	Hour	Summary of Events and Information	Remarks and references to Appendices
LINE.	21-11-17		Hostile Artillery was very quiet except near our forward guns which were subjected to heavy fire. An Enemy M.G. swept OAK AVENUE apparently firing from LOCK V. The weather was again unsuitable for aerial reconnaissance - consequently there was no activity. Emplacements were remade. A new position was taken up in the SUPPORT LINE from which it was possible to engage GAME COPSE – a sphere of Enemy movement and apparently a strong point. 1000 rounds were fired into GAME COPSE – Enemy artillery retaliated 2000 – – – – – BASSEVILLE WOOD	
	22-11-17		Slight intermittent hostile artillery activity. No casualties, no damage to gun positions or dug outs. Hostile Aircraft was inactive – one hostile balloon was observed at 8.10am. – 142°M. from 135 a. 40.15. More ammunition was taken to near the gun positions and a new covered emplacement was commenced. During the night 9000 rounds were fired on enemy tracks in P7c 0.12 b. and LOCK V. A hostile M.G. was silenced at LOCK V.	

D. D. & L., London, E.C.
(A8001) Wt. W1771/M2031 750,000 5/17 Sch. 52 Forms/C2118/14

Instructions regarding War Diaries and Intelligence Summaries are contained in F. S. Regs., Part II. and the Staff Manual respectively. Title pages will be prepared in manuscript.

WAR DIARY
or
INTELLIGENCE SUMMARY.
(Erase heading not required.)

Army Form C. 2118.

Place	Date	Hour	Summary of Events and Information	Remarks and references to Appendices
LINE.	23.11.17		Hostile artillery on the whole was very quiet. Between 11 and 12 noon the enemy heavily shelled the area O.4.b and O.5.c. Two hostile aeroplanes flew over our lines at 10.0 a.m. but were soon driven off by anti-aircraft fire. In accordance with a suspected enemy relief our guns were very active during the night – a much heavier harassing fire being maintained on tracks supposed to be used by him during relief and on other known routes of movement. 18,000 rounds were fired on tracks in P.7.c 1000 – – – – LOCK V. 8500 – – – – P2b. 50-75. and P.7.a.	
	24.11.17		Hostile artillery was very active – RAVINE, TRANSPORT CORNER – BLUFF, BOW H.Q. and CHATEAU WOOD receiving great attention. Hostile aircraft – inactive. Two aeroplanes (apparently British) were seen to collide at 3.0 p.m. and both 'planes crashed in the neighbourhood of SHREWSBURY FOREST. 3 hostile balloons were observed during the day. Harassing fire maintained – 11,500 rounds expended.	

D. D. & L., London, E.C.
(A8001) Wt. W1771/M2031 750,000 5/17 Sch. 52 Forms/C2118/14

Instructions regarding War Diaries and Intelligence Summaries are contained in F. S. Regs., Part II. and the Staff Manual respectively. Title pages will be prepared in manuscript.

WAR DIARY
or
INTELLIGENCE SUMMARY.
(Erase heading not required.)

Army Form C. 2118.

Place	Date	Hour	Summary of Events and Information	Remarks and references to Appendices
LINE.	25.11.17		A daylight relief (inter company) was carried out, commencing 2.0 pm. Relief was complete by 4 30 pm. Hostile artillery shelled intermittently FUSILIER WOOD, THE RAVINE, TRANSPORT CORNER, CHATEAU WOOD being attended to. Hostile Aircraft came over our lines in large numbers and again later in the day. Two new emplacements, splinter proof completed. Harassing fire was carried out throughout the night, 4500 rounds being fired on Tracks and dugouts.	
	26.11.17		Very slight hostile artillery activity. Aircraft inactive. Routine work was carried out during the day whilst at night our harassing fire was brought to bear on LOCK V. and Tracks. — 6000 rounds expended.	
	27.11.17		Hostile Artillery was far more active than usual — the following areas being shelled. CHATEAU WOOD — 500 FUSILIER do 20. BATTLE do 20	

D. D. & L., London, E.C.
(A8001) Wt. W1771/M2031 750,000 5/17 Sch. 52 Forms/C2118/14

Instructions regarding War Diaries and Intelligence Summaries are contained in F. S. Regs., Part II. and the Staff Manual respectively. Title pages will be prepared in manuscript.

WAR DIARY
or
INTELLIGENCE SUMMARY.
(Erase heading not required.)

Army Form C. 2118.

Place	Date	Hour	Summary of Events and Information	Remarks and references to Appendices
LINE.	27.11.17		A hostile M.G. was active - from GAME COPSE.	
			Harassing fire was maintained on Dugouts, Tracks etc	
			7000 rounds expended.	
	28.11.17		Hostile Artillery very active - area shoot	
			- Aircraft inactive.	
			Routine work was carried out.	
			The Transport lines moved from BUTTERFLY FARM to BAROSSA CAMP.	
			6500 rounds were fired during the night - 5000 of which were fired on ground suspected to be strongly patrolled by the Enemy. LAMB F^m, and WIND COTTS also received attention from us. Emplacements were improved.	
	29.11.17		Hostile Artillery showed normal activity special attention being paid to CHATEAU WOOD, FUSILIER WOOD, IMPERIAL WALK + AVENUE.	
			Two Enemy aircraft were observed flying high over CHATEAU WOOD	
			Harassing fire was energetically carried out by us on tracks used by the Enemy and in the region of HOLLEBEKE CHATEAU.	

Instructions regarding War Diaries and Intelligence Summaries are contained in F. S. Regs., Part II. and the Staff Manual respectively. Title pages will be prepared in manuscript.

WAR DIARY
or
INTELLIGENCE SUMMARY.
(Erase heading not required.)

Army Form C. 2118.

Place	Date	Hour	Summary of Events and Information	Remarks and references to Appendices
LINE.	29.11.17		20 of the Enemy were seen about O. 12 a. 80.40. Gas gongs were placed at each dugout and gas blankets installed	
	30.11.17		Hostile Artillery was fairly active during the day and especially during the night, FUSILIER WOOD, BATTLE WOOD, OAF + IMPERIAL AVENUES Enemy aircraft was more active than usual whilst our own 'planes were also very active. It is ascertained that the Enemy is using the road from O 12 b 90.45 to O 12 b 20.80 and to Lock V. One man was returned to the Transport Lines - Sick. Our harassing fire during the night was greatly increased owing to our Cooperation with the Artillery on a position upon which the Enemy is hard at work - POOL FARM to dugouts J. 32 d. 75. 32. 20000 rounds were expended. KIND COTTS, TROOM FARM Tracks etc. being harassed throughout the night. New gun positions in 136 b. were reconnoitred and completed	E[illegible] 207 M G Coy

D. D. & L., London, E.C. (A8001) Wt. W1771/M2031 750,000 5/17 Sch. 52 Forms/C2118/14

372

Army Form C. 2118.

Instructions regarding War Diaries and Intelligence Summaries are contained in F. S. Regs., Part II. and the Staff Manual respectively. Title pages will be prepared in manuscript.

WAR DIARY
or
INTELLIGENCE SUMMARY.
(Erase heading not required.)

247 Co

10

Place	Date	Hour	Summary of Events and Information	Remarks and references to Appendices
LINE	1/12/17		Enemy artillery less active than usual, OAF AVENUE, OAK DUMP, BOW DUGOUTS, WHITE CHATEAU WOOD and OAK SUPPORT were shelled a little. Our aircraft fairly active during afternoon, enemy's not in evidence. Hostile M.G. bullets reaching vicinity of BOW DUGOUTS from THE TWINS. Harassing fire carried out on ROAD JUNCT. P7 a 8.4 + PUMP FARM, 2500 rounds being expended. Trench mountings built into barrage positions 11-14 guns. Track connecting IMPERIAL DUGOUTS with OAF AVENUE improved. Stand made for sentries post. Entrance to AID POST improved + latrine reconstructed + improved. Alternative emplacements completed for 1 + 2 guns. No 1 team salved 10 boxes S.A.A. from WHITE CHATEAU WOOD + carried to position. No 89407 Pte A. E. ALLEN sent to hospital.	
	2/12/17		Enemy artillery quiet, HILL 60, WHITE CHATEAU WOOD and OAK SUPPORT receiving a little attention. No aerial activity. Company relief carried out in order. Harassing fire maintained during night on ROAD JUNCT. P7 a 8.4 + TRACKS on O.12 d 70.73; No of rounds S.A.A. fired: 2000. 11-14 guns moved from barrage positions at I36 a 33.00 to emplacements at I36 b 7.3. 4 new night firing screens made for 11-14 guns. No 1 + 2 guns alternative emplacements improved.	③
	3/12/17		Enemy artillery fairly quiet, OAF AVENUE, WHITE CHATEAU WOOD + OAK SUPPORT shelled a little. Hostile aircraft fairly active during night dropping bombs on back areas behind DEHBSKE FARM. In conjunction with push on POLDEHOEK CHATEAU 11-14 guns at I36 b 7 3 put down a barrage on PACK, LONG + KENT FARMS from noon to 1 p.m., when guns were withdrawn singly and [illegible] on S.O.S. lines at barrage positions I36 a 33.00. 13000 rounds of S.A.A. were expended + after 40 minutes firing the enemy shelled about the position with 4.2s and continued after guns were withdrawn. During the night harassing fire was continued on enemy centres of work + movement viz TUBE CROSS RDS P8 a 3 8 ROAD JUNCT P7 a 8.4, 4500 rounds S.A.A. being expended. All dugouts cleaned + baled out. R.E. helped with canteen at I36 c 2 8.	
	4/12/17		[illegible] heavy hostile shelling of OAF AVENUE, TRANSPORT CORNER, OAK SUPPORT and WHITE CHATEAU WOOD. Enemy aircraft again bombed our back areas during night. M.G. from the TWINS against [illegible] 1 + 2 positions. We continued harassing fire on enemy centres of movement, viz:	

D. D. & L., London, E.C. (A6013) Wt. W 1771/M2031 750,000 3/17 Sch. 52 Forms/C2118/14

WAR DIARY
or
INTELLIGENCE SUMMARY.
(Erase heading not required.)

Army Form C. 2118.

Instructions regarding War Diaries and Intelligence Summaries are contained in F. S. Regs., Part II. and the Staff Manual respectively. Title pages will be prepared in manuscript.

373

Place	Date	Hour	Summary of Events and Information	Remarks and references to Appendices
LINE	4/12/17	(m.H.)	CHALK FARM, BASSEVILLE CABT & HOLLEBEKE CHATEAU RD S of CHATEAU FM in P7a. 9000 rounds S.A.A. being expended.	
			Right note: C.O. gave permission for his wire to be tapped, so that we could connect Coy HQ in SPOIL BANK with Bn H.Q. at AID POST, provided we have a Fullerphone. This was done.	
			32 boxes S.A.A. carried from TRANSPORT CORNER to 11-14 positions I 36 a 33 00. R.Es helped with Canteen at I.36 C 2 8.	
"	5/12/17		Enemy artillery very active on OAF & IMPERIAL AVENUES, FUSILIER & WHITE CHATEAU WOODS. Much aerial activity.	
			Harassing fire carried out on TRACKS in P7c & PUMP FM, 7000 rounds in all. Ravine cleaned up, all dugouts cleaned & baled.	
"	6/12/17		Enemy artillery active on OAF AV, FUSILIER & WHITE CHATEAU WOODS & TRANSPORT CORNER. Aircraft active. Harassing fire on CHALK FM, BASSEVILLE CABT & ROAD JUNCT P7a 8 4, 6000 rounds in all.	
			All dugouts cleaned & baled. Salvage. No 115483, Pte CLARK P. sent to hospital.	
	7/12/17		Enemy artillery fairly quiet, OAF & IMPERIAL AVENUES & WHITE CHATEAU WOODS shelled a little. Own aircraft active, 1 brought down by A.A. fire at 2.50 p.m. Enemy not in evidence.	
			Harassing fire on TRACKS in P7c, SUNKEN RD near BASSEVILLE CABT & ROAD JUNCT P7a 8 4; 16000 rounds S.A.A. expended in all.	
			2 new firing screens made at 11-14 position & entrance to cookhouse there strengthened.	
"	8/12/17		Enemy artillery fairly quiet, a little shelling of WHITE CHATEAU WOOD, FUSILIER & BATTLE WOODS. Own aircraft very active, but few enemy planes seen.	
			Harassing fire was carried out during the night on centres of enemy movement at TUBE CROSS RDS, DEVILS ELBOW, PIE FARM & P7a 8 4 to P1 d 0 2, 10000 rounds being fired.	
			All dugouts cleaned & baled.	
			Salvage carried to dump.	

D. D. & L., London, E.C.
(A8031) Wt. W1771/M2031 750,000 5/17 Sch. 52 Forms/C2118/14

Army Form C. 2118.

WAR DIARY
or
INTELLIGENCE SUMMARY.
(Erase heading not required.)

Instructions regarding War Diaries and Intelligence Summaries are contained in F. S. Regs., Part II. and the Staff Manual respectively. Title pages will be prepared in manuscript.

374

Place	Date	Hour	Summary of Events and Information	Remarks and references to Appendices
LINE	9/12/17		Hostile artillery was moderately active on FUSILIER WOOD, OAF AVENUE and WHITE CHATEAU Wood. There was no aerial activity. Enemy sniping round 3 + 4 positions (in front of OAK SUPPORT). Harassing fire was carried out on DEVILS ELBOW, EAST FARM and ROAD from P.7 a 40.38 to P.7 a 70.40, 5000 rounds S.A.A. being expended. All dugouts were cleaned + baled out, and RAVINE in FUSILIER WOOD cleaned up. An inter-Company relief was carried out, the outgoing Sections (3 + 4) going direct to C CAMP RIDGE WOOD (N 5 b.) for work under C.R.E., instead of to BAROSSA CAMP (Transport Lines).	
"	10/12/17		Enemy artillery fairly active on OAF AVENUE, FUSILIER, BATTLE + WHITE CHATEAU WOODS, and CANAL BANK from OLD IRON BRIDGE to BOW H.Q. Own aircraft busy all day, enemy also active, 12 flying low over FUSILIER WOOD at 1 p.m., + a large GOTHA over BATTLE WOOD at 3 p.m. Much enemy movement observed round TROON FM, CHALK FM, PIN HOUSE, DAMP COPSE + PIE FARM. Enemy smoke barrage seen behind their front line 10° left of HERVICG CHURCH from No 1 gun (O 10 b. 56.65). Harassing fire carried out on TRACKS in P.7c + SUNKEN RD near BASSEVILLE CABT (P.2 b.); 7500 rounds fired. New latrines were built at Nos 1 + 2 positions. Work commenced by 3 + 4 Sections + details at RIDGEWOOD CAMP under C.R.E., draining of Camp, construction of duckboard tracks, demolition of obsolete dugouts, etc.	
"	11/12/17		Enemy artillery fairly quiet. HILL 60, OAF AVENUE, FUSILIER WOOD (gas) and WHITE CHATEAU WOOD were shelled a little. No aerial activity. Enemy M.G. fired at intervals through FUSILIER WOOD from EAST FARM. 3 + 4 positions also subjected to sniping from M.Gs + rifles. During night 3 + 4 teams withdrawn from positions in front of OAK SUPPORT as follows:– No 3 team to mine at O 5 c 78.22. S.O.S. line laid out + given to team. " 4 " " Sub H.Q. preparatory to taking up position in THE BLUFF at O 5 b 68.60. We carried out harassing fire on TRACKS used by enemy in P.7 c, 1000 rounds S.A.A. being	

D. D. & L., London, E.C.
(A5005) Wt. W1771/M2031 750,000 5/17 Sch. 52 Forms C2118/14

Instructions regarding War Diaries and Intelligence Summaries are contained in F. S. Regs., Part II. and the Staff Manual respectively. Title pages will be prepared in manuscript.

WAR DIARY
or
INTELLIGENCE SUMMARY.

(Erase heading not required.)

Army Form C. 2118.

Place	Date	Hour	Summary of Events and Information 375	Remarks and references to Appendices
LINE	11/12/17 (Cont'd)		expended.	
			Dugout cleaned + pumped out. Range Cards + Orders for 11-14 guns made out again. New position for No 3 about O 5 c 78 22 reconnoitred.	
"	12/12/17		Hostile artillery fairly quiet, except on WHITE CHATEAU WOOD, which was rather heavily bombarded at intervals. Much aerial activity on both sides; enemy dropped bombs near TRANSPORT CORNER + SANDBAG BRIDGE. Hostile M.G. fired over FUSILIER WOOD from GAME CORPSE.	
			We carried out harassing fire on enemy's tracks in P 7 c. expending 10,000 rounds S.A.A.	
			Ramps in FUSILIER WOOD cleaned out. No 4 gun moved to THE BLUFF (O 5 b 68.60) + team moved into tunnel there. S.O.S line laid out from tunnel entrance on Canal side. Team commenced work on draining pillbox at end of BLUFF. Position reconnoitred.	
"	13/12/17		Enemy artillery quiet, desultory shelling of BATTLE + FUSILIER WOODS. No aerial activity. Enemy M.G. firing through FUSILIER WOOD from GAME CORPSE + through WHITE CHATEAU WOOD from LOCK 5.	
			We fired during the night on PIE FARM + TUBE CROSS RDS. 5000 rounds.	
			No 4 team digging trench from + draining pillbox at end of BLUFF. 20 boxes S.A.A. + W. belt boxes [illegible] in FUSILIER WOOD.	
	14/12/17		Enemy artillery fairly quiet, a little shelling of THE BLUFF, HILL 60, FUSILIER + WHITE CHATEAU WOODS. No aerial activity. Hostile M.G. again firing over WHITE CHATEAU WOOD from LOCK 5. A fire seen in ZANDVOORDE at 9.15 p.m. A hostile patrol attempted to raid No 1 infantry post in HOLLEBEKE at 2.30 a.m. One of our men died of wounds but no prisoners were lost.	
			Harassing fire was carried out on DEVIL'S ELBOW, EAST FARM and enemy TRACKS in P 7 c, 6000 rounds fired.	
			New S.O.S posts put out + emplacements altered. 30 boxes S.A.A. carried from TRANSPORT CORNER to FUSILIER WOOD. Pillbox in BLUFF drained as low as possible + trench finished.	

D. D. & L., London, E.C. (A5000) Wt. W2771/M2031 750,000 5/17 Sch. 52 Forms/C2118/14

Instructions regarding War Diaries and Intelligence Summaries are contained in F. S. Regs., Part II. and the Staff Manual respectively. Title pages will be prepared in manuscript.

WAR DIARY
or
INTELLIGENCE SUMMARY.
(Erase heading not required.)

Army Form C. 2118.

376

Place	Date	Hour	Summary of Events and Information	Remarks and references to Appendices
LINE.	15/11/17.		Enemy artillery fairly active on TRANSPORT CORNER, IMPERIAL AVENUE, FUSILIER and WHITE CHATEAU WOODS. No aerial activity. M.G. again firing across WHITE CHATEAU WOOD. Company relief carried out in order. Harassing fire maintained during night on centres of enemy movement, P.2.a 90.95, POOL FARM, P.2.b 9.7 to P.2.b 15.75, CHATEAU FM. & TRACKS in P.7.c. 8000 rounds fired.	
	16/11/17		Enemy artillery rather harassing, shelling IMPERIAL AVENUE, HILL 60, FUSILIER WOOD and BLUFF BANK at intervals. Own & hostile aircraft much in evidence. Enemy M.G. fired over FUSILIER & WHITE CHATEAU WOODS. Harassing fire continued on centres of enemy movement, P.2.b.10.75, BASSEVILLE CABT. & ROAD JUNCT P.7.a 8.4, 5000 rounds. New platforms made at No 1 position. Gun recesses made for 2, 13 & 14 guns. Draining continued at No 6 position pillbox.	
	17/11/17		Enemy artillery exceptionally quiet. No aerial activity. Enemy M.G. harassed 13 & 14 positions during night. Harassing fire carried out on centres of enemy work & movement) in cooperation with artillery (dummy raid). ROAD P.7.a.8.6 to P.1.c.9.0. MAY FM. & GAME COPSE. 15000 rounds being expended. All dugouts cleaned & drained.	
	18/11/17		Enemy artillery active on HILL 60, TRANSPORT CORNER, FUSILIER & WHITE CHATEAU WOODS. Aircraft lively, one British came down apparently in no man's land. 2 enemy planes were [illegible] at 3.45 p.m. over WHITE CHATEAU WOOD. The following centres of enemy movement were harassed by M.G. fire: P.2.c.3.7, P.2.a 75.00 to 80.50, P.2.b.10.75, P.1.c.55.18, TROON FM. & TRACKS in P.7.c. 11000 rounds fired in all. Duckboard track from IMPERIAL DUGOUTS to OAF AVENUE improved. Trench at No 4 position pillbox deepened. Lt. MONCAR (4 Sect) slightly wounded. Carried on duty after inoculation.	

D. D. & L., London, E.C.
(A5001) Wt. W1771/M2031 750,000 5/17 Sch. 52 Forms C2118/14

Instructions regarding War Diaries and Intelligence Summaries are contained in F. S. Regs., Part II. and the Staff Manual respectively. Title pages will be prepared in manuscript.

WAR DIARY
or
INTELLIGENCE SUMMARY.
(Erase heading not required.)

Army Form C. 2118.

37

Place	Date	Hour	Summary of Events and Information	Remarks and references to Appendices
LINE.	19/12/17.		Enemy artillery active on TRANSPORT CORNER, FUSILIER WOOD + RAVINE, BLUFF and WHITE CHATEAU WOOD. 10 p.m. – 12 p.m. gas shells on WHITE CHATEAU WOOD + on our left. Enemy T.Ms fired on THE BLUFF at intervals throughout the night, + a machine gun through WHITE CHATEAU WOOD. Aircraft fairly active on both sides. Fire from our guns was brought to bear on centres of enemy movement in co-operation with artillery (dummy raid) as foll:- P7 a 8.6 to P1 c 9.0 (ROAD), P2 a 75.00, MAY FM. + GAME COPSE. 15000 rounds were fired. Dugout for 11-14 guns in RAVINE improved. Positions for these guns for direct fire in event of further barrage fire being ineffective selected close to SIGHT HOUSE in I 36 c.	
"	20/12/17.		Enemy artillery below normal. Desultory shelling of IMPERIAL AVENUE, FUSILIER WOOD, BLUFF (gas). Enemy M.G. again firing across WHITE CHATEAU WOOD. Harassing fire by our guns on centres of enemy movement at P2 c 3.7, P2 a 7.5 to 8.5, P2 b 9.7 to 15.75, P13 a 30.65 + P1 c 55.18. 14000 rounds expended. New emplacement for 11 gun commenced at I 36 a 33.02, + work commenced on direct fire emplacements for 11-14 guns at I 36 c 82.81, 75.92, 82.95 + 81.99.	
"	21/12/17.		Enemy artillery more active on OAF AVENUE, FUSILIER + WHITE CHATEAU WOODS; gas also employed on last two localities. Little aerial activity. Enemy M.G. very active over WHITE CHAT. WOOD. Harassing fire carried out on following centres of enemy movement:- P2 c 3.7, P2 a 7.5 to 8.5, SPUD FM, JUNCT. of TRACKS at O 12 d 73.74, 9000 rounds being fired. The last-named drew enemy M.G. + artillery fire in retaliation. A fire was observed in enemy's lines at ZANDVOORDE from 1-2.30 a.m. Salvage + routine work carried on. Pte. BURGOYNE (No. 4 Sect.) sent to hospital with trench fever.	

D. D. & L., London, E.C.
(A6021) Wt. W1771/M2031 750,000 3/17 Sch. 52 Forms/C2118/14

WAR DIARY
or
INTELLIGENCE SUMMARY.

(Erase heading not required.)

Instructions regarding War Diaries and Intelligence Summaries are contained in F. S. Regs., Part II. and the Staff Manual respectively. Title pages will be prepared in manuscript.

Army Form C. 2118.

378

Place	Date	Hour	Summary of Events and Information	Remarks and references to Appendices
LINE.	22/12/17		Enemy artillery was exceptionally active from 9 a.m. to 1 p.m. over all parts. Subsequently fairly quiet, THE BLUFF, FUSILIER WOOD and WHITE CHATEAU WOOD being shelled a little at intervals. Own & enemy aircraft fairly active in afternoon. Harassing fire was carried out on centres of enemy movement at P2 c 3.7, J32 d 38.18, CROSS ROADS at P2 b 15.75, TRACKS in P7c & LOCK 5, 7000 rounds of S.A.A. being expended. Possible retaliation on FUSILIER WOOD between 10 p.m. & 6 a.m., during which time gas shells were sent over at intervals. Company relief carried out in order.	
"	23/12/17		Enemy artillery moderately active on THE BLUFF, FUSILIER & WHITE CHATEAU WOODS at intervals. Enemy M.G. harassed positions in WHITE CHATEAU WOOD from THE TWINS. Much aerial activity. At 3.20 p.m. 1 enemy plane was brought down by one of our scouts, falling in HESSIAN WOOD, where it burst into flames. A few gas shells on BATTLE WOOD, nose cap of one found, marked EK17, EG17, 290 d. Harassing fire was carried out on an area which would be used by the enemy during a probable relief. Targets P1 c 9.2, P13 a 3.0, P2 c 65.75 to P2 c 40.25, 16000 rounds being fired. New S.O.S. & Switch Charts, also Range Cards were made out for 11-14 guns. 3 S.O.S. mortars & 3 rifle grenades received at IMPERIAL DUGOUTS for repeating S.O.S. signal from front line, & orders for their use added to Sentries orders	
"	24/12/17		Enemy artillery fairly active on OAK SUPPORT, WHITE CHATEAU WOOD, BLUFF & IMPERIAL DUGOUTS. No aerial activity. Enemy M.G. firing over 11-14 positions, & also No 4 in THE BLUFF. Harassing fire carried out on centres of enemy movement at P2 a 88.20, P7 a 00.80, P7 a 20.75, 4000 rounds being fired. This drew retaliation with 77 m/m & gas shells. Two new emplacements made for 11 & 14 guns. Work commenced to drain flooded dugout at 13 b a 4.00. Tunnelling work carried on in BLUFF BANK.	
"	25/12/17		Much smoke was seen rising in KORTEWILDE at 8 a.m. Our artillery was very active, enemy's moderate BATTLE & WHITE CHATEAU WOODS, BLUFF BANK & OAK SUPPORT receiving attention. No aerial activity. Enemy M.G. fired on No 1 & 2 positions from LOCK 5. Harassing fire continued on P7 a 00.80 & P7 a 20.75, 2000 rounds of S.A.A. being expended.	

D. D. & L., London, E.C. (A8001) Wt. W1771/M2031 750,000 5/17 Sch. 52 Forms/C2118/14

Instructions regarding War Diaries and Intelligence Summaries are contained in F. S. Regs., Part II. and the Staff Manual respectively. Title pages will be prepared in manuscript.

WAR DIARY
or
INTELLIGENCE SUMMARY.
(Erase heading not required.)

Army Form C. 2118.

379

Place	Date	Hour	Summary of Events and Information	Remarks and references to Appendices
LINE	25/12/17	(Contd)	Draining of flooded dugout in FUSILIER WOOD (I36a 40.00) continued & trench dug. Direction board received from Brigade marked with limits of [illegible] front, & given to Sentry (11-14 positions). Direction sticks placed out for this purpose.	
"	26/12/17		Enemy artillery was fairly active on FUSILIER & WHITE CHATEAU WOODS, BLUFF BANK, OAK AVENUE & SUPPORT LINE. A number of gas shells were sent over. Aircraft a good deal in evidence, both ours & hostile. Enemy sniper fired over 11-14 positions from just beyond GRAVES COPSE & on OAK SUPPORT from LOCK 6. Enemy M.G. firing over No 7 position from THE TWINS. We harassed enemy centres of movement at P7a 2.4 to P7a 8.4 & P7a 17.25, firing 6000 rounds. Work continued on trench from flooded dugout at I36a 4.0. Sump at AID POST (Bn H.Q.) pumped out. Positions forward at O5b 60.20 & O5b 75.35 (A & B positions) reconnoitred for accommodation for [illegible] teams. Sticks put out for S.O.S. [illegible] for these positions as follows:— A. True bearing 116° Q.E. 1°15' } traverse 2° left & 2° right. S.O.S. [illegible] P7a 20.98 B. " 102° " 0°45' } P7a 20.90	
	27/12/17		Enemy artillery very harassing, distributing a large number of gas & H.E. shells over OAK SUPPORT, CANAL WALK, WHITE CHATEAU & FUSILIER WOODS. Own aircraft fairly active during the day, [illegible] enemy over about 6 p.m. Enemy sniping 11-14 positions from HOLLEBEKE CHATEAU & BLUFF BANK from LOCK 6 (M.G.). Harassing fire carried out on P7a 2.4 to P7a 8.4 (ROAD) and P2c 45.38 to P2c 65.75 (ROAD), 5000 rounds being expended. This drew 77 m/m & gas shells in retaliation. Teams manned A & B positions & guns laid as above. Trench from flooded dugout at I36a 4.0 completed. 11-14 teams turned out four times during night and each time were [illegible] S.O.S. lines in under 2 mins. Sections & details out of the line left C CAMP, RIDGEWOOD and returned to BAROSSA CAMP (Transport Lines).	

D. D. & L., London, E.C. (A8012) Wt. W1771/M2031 750,000 5/17 Sch. 52 Forms/C2118/14

Instructions regarding War Diaries and Intelligence Summaries are contained in F. S. Regs., Part II. and the Staff Manual respectively. Title pages will be prepared in manuscript.

WAR DIARY
or
INTELLIGENCE SUMMARY.

(Erase heading not required.)

Army Form C. 2118.

Place	Date	Hour	Summary of Events and Information	Remarks and references to Appendices
			381	
LINE	31/12/17		Hostile artillery moderately active on WHITE CHATEAU + FUSILIER WOODS + OAF AVENUE. Little aerial activity.	
			The following centres of enemy activity were harassed by our M. Gs. – P7c 60.75 and TRACKS in that locality, P7c 1.3, TUBE CROSS + PIE FARM, 12000 rounds, S.A.A. being expended.	
			Tunnelling continued in BLUFF BANK. RAVINE in FUSILIER WOOD cleared up.	
			Serg Holtwood C. & Cpl Cropper H.A. transferred from this Company to 20th Div.	
			31. 12. 17.	
			E Matthew Taylor 2/Lt for OC. 247 M. G. Coy.	

247 M.G. COY.

Sheet. 1.

Army Form C. 2118.

WAR DIARY
or
INTELLIGENCE SUMMARY.

(Erase heading not required.)

Instructions regarding War Diaries and Intelligence Summaries are contained in F. S. Regs., Part II. and the Staff Manual respectively. Title pages will be prepared in manuscript.

Place	Date	Hour	Summary of Events and Information	Remarks and references to Appendices
LINE E. of HOLLEBEKE	Jan. 1 1918.		The two Sections in the line spent the greater portion of the day in improving and strengthening existing gun Emplacements and in transferring ammunition from the dumps to the gun positions. Ammunition was carried to the No 2 Gun position in the BLUFF. At night our Machine Guns activity was somewhat increased and hostile tracks in P.7.c.1.3, P.7.c.60.63, PIE F^m, and TUBE CROSS ROADS received great attention. 18,000 rounds were Expended.	
			ARTILLERY. The Artilleries of both Sides were more active than is usual, due no doubt to the occasion - the Commencement of the New Year. The hostile Shelling was Spasmodic and occasionally heavy.	
			RAILWAY TRENCH, OAF AVENUE, IMPERIAL AVENUE, + THE RAVINE, received his attention	
			AIRCRAFT. The activity was below normal. One Enemy Aeroplane crossed our lines at 5.0 pm and again later in the Evening. No apparent Signals.	
			During the night the activity of Hostile Machine Guns was above normal - CHATEAU WOOD receiving attention. The light Signals of the Enemy were normal	

D. D. & L., London, E.C.
(A7883) Wt. W807/M1672 350,000 4/17 Sch. 52a Forms/C/2118/14

Sheet. 2.

Army Form C. 2118.

Instructions regarding War Diaries and Intelligence Summaries are contained in F. S. Regs., Part II. and the Staff Manual respectively. Title pages will be prepared in manuscript.

WAR DIARY
or
INTELLIGENCE SUMMARY.
(Erase heading not required.)

Place	Date	Hour	Summary of Events and Information	Remarks and references to Appendices
LINE	2-1-18		The ground was still ice-bound but the day quite clear and the sun shone making visibility very good. One Gun detailed as a sniping gun was put in position and two gun teams were taken to the direct fire Emplacements. The tunnel at the BLUFF was made, the only requirements now being a staircase & platform.	
			ARTILLERY :- Our artillery was active throughout the day.	
		4.30 a.m	Hostile artillery was very active throughout the day. Intermittent shelling of :- BATTLE WOOD, TRANSPORT CORNER, ~~on~~ RAVINE and CHATEAU WOOD. About 4.30 am the Enemy shelled CHATEAU WOOD, the CANAL BANK and BDE H.Q. very heavily with gas shells. Gun teams at No 2 Position were obliged to wear their box respirators for twenty minutes.	
		8.45 pm.	At 8.45 pm. S.O.S. went up on the Sector on our left. Our Artillery and Machine Guns opened out and fired at various intervals during the night. Hostile artillery heavily bombarded the Sector on our left then settled down to ordinary harassing fire. At 4.30 am he opened out again on our right and on CHATEAU WOOD - 5.9s 4.2s and gas shells being used.	
			Our Machine Guns were more than normally active, 14000 rounds being expended on Enemy tracks, BASSEVILLE CABt and the road to the South of it.	

D. D. & L., London, E.C.
(A7883) Wt. W80/M1672 350,000 4/17 Sch. 52a Forms/C/2118/14

Instructions regarding War Diaries and Intelligence Summaries are contained in F. S. Regs., Part II. and the Staff Manual respectively. Title pages will be prepared in manuscript.

WAR DIARY
or
INTELLIGENCE SUMMARY.
(Erase heading not required.)

Army Form C. 2118.

Place	Date	Hour	Summary of Events and Information	Remarks and references to Appendices
LINE	2.1.18		Hostile Machine Guns continued in their abnormal activity – No 1 and 4 positions being in the line of fire. The hostile gun firing against No 1 team was reported to have moved from its previous position.	
			Aircraft – both our own and the Enemy were very active throughout the day. Two balloons were observed.	
	3.1.18.		There was a thaw during the day making the ground fairly soft. The visibility was poor & misty. The Platform required in the position in the BLUFF was commenced. The Sniping position was camouflaged and the emplacement slightly deepened to allow the tripod to sit better.	
			13500 rounds were expended on tracks, PIG Fm, TUBE CROSS ROADS. whilst from 7.15 – 7.45 the barrage guns were switched on to 'A' Switch – a practice switch. Fire was opened three minutes after receiving word.	
			ARTILLERY. Our artillery was active throughout the day and night.	
			Hostile artillery activity was much more than normal.	
			TRANSPORT CORNER, RAILWAY TRENCH, THE RAVINE and WHITE CHATEAU were his targets – Several direct hits on the duck board track through the wood.	

D. D. & L., London, E.C. (A7883) Wt. W807/M1672 350,000 4/17 Sch. 52a Forms/C/2118/14

Sheet. 4. Army Form C. 2118.

WAR DIARY
or
INTELLIGENCE SUMMARY.
(Erase heading not required.)

Instructions regarding War Diaries and Intelligence Summaries are contained in F. S. Regs., Part II. and the Staff Manual respectively. Title pages will be prepared in manuscript.

Place	Date	Hour	Summary of Events and Information	Remarks and references to Appendices
LINE	3.1.18		From 4.30 am to 6.0 am the Enemy shelled BOW H.Q. and through CHATEAU WOOD and caused the camouflage to be burnt. He used a great number of Gas Shells and the team at No 1 Position were compelled to wear Box Respirators for two hours.	
			Our heavy artillery then became very active and Enemy dumps were observed to be alight - one at 6.15 p.m. - the other at 3.15 a.m.	
			The Australian M.G. H.Q. was visited and S.O.S. lines compared to ensure overlapping.	
			Hostile Machine Guns were singularly inactive during the period under review. Our barrage gun positions in FUSILIER WOOD were nearly hit.	
			AIRCRAFT. Seven of our 'planes were observed over FUSILIER WOOD at 10.0 am.	
			Enemy 'planes were observed over FUSILIER WOOD between 6.30 am and 7.0 am and artillery fire was opened out by the Enemy.	
			Two hostile balloons were observed but they remained up only a short time due probably to the poor visibility afforded by the mists.	
			There were no Casualties caused by Enemy artillery activity.	

D. D. & L., London, E.C.
(A7883) Wt. W80/M1672 350,000 4/17 Sch. 52a Forms/C/2118/14

Sheet 5.

Army Form C. 2118.

Instructions regarding War Diaries and Intelligence Summaries are contained in F. S. Regs., Part II. and the Staff Manual respectively. Title pages will be prepared in manuscript.

WAR DIARY
or
INTELLIGENCE SUMMARY.
(Erase heading not required.)

Place	Date	Hour	Summary of Events and Information	Remarks and references to Appendices
LINE.	Jan. 4th 1918.		Early morning misty and remained so until 10.0 am. when the visibility became good. The ground hard and icebound in the morning became soft when the thaw commenced. Work was continued in the BLUFF TUNNEL POSITION and the position nearly completed and ready for occupation. The usual routine was carried out.	
			MACHINE GUNS. - Our guns were not quite so active as usual. The fire of our No 1 Guns drew retaliatory fire from an Enemy M.G. - no damage.	
			Hostile Machine Guns were quieter than usual - one gun firing in the direction of the Dugout occupied by the BARRAGE GUN TEAMS in FUSILIER WOOD.	
			We fired 13000 rounds on LOCK 5, tracks in P.7.c, P7b, and P1.d.	
			ARTILLERY. Our artillery was active throughout the day and the night. Our guns shelled heavily between 8.0 pm. and 9.30 pm.	
			Hostile artillery was also active throughout the period under review: BATTLE WOOD, TRANSPORT CORNER, and IMPERIAL AVENUE receiving special attention.	
			At 5.0 pm. the enemy bombarded the region above for a period of 5 minutes.	
			No casualties were suffered by us.	

D. D. & L., London, E.C. (A7883) Wt. W803/M1672 350,000 4/17 Sch. 52a Forms/C/2118/14

Sheet. 6.

Army Form C. 2118.

WAR DIARY
or
INTELLIGENCE SUMMARY.
(Erase heading not required.)

Instructions regarding War Diaries and Intelligence Summaries are contained in F. S. Regs., Part II. and the Staff Manual respectively. Title pages will be prepared in manuscript.

Place	Date	Hour	Summary of Events and Information	Remarks and references to Appendices
LINE.	4.1.18		AIRCRAFT. Two of our aeroplanes crossed the enemy lines during the morning. Our planes	
	contd		were active day and night. Enemy searchlight seen to be used against our	
			planes by night. One E.A. was brought down and fell behind the	
			enemy lines. At 8.0 pm. an enemy plane was observed over our	
			support lines.	
			During the day 8 hostile balloons were observed.	
			No. 1 + 2 Sections relieved No. 3 and 4 Sections the latter returning to T. lines.	
do.	5-1-18		This day was fine and cold, the ground very hard and slippery whilst the visibility	
			was only moderate.	
			Machine Guns:- 10,500 rounds were fired by us on the following targets - LOCK 4 and	
			on enemy tracks in O.18.b. 25.70, I36a 33.00, I36 a. 34.08 and P2c. 0.2.	
			Hostile Machine Gun fire was normal. No. 1, 2 + 3 gun teams reported	
			hostile machine gun bullets to be passing overhead.	
			ARTILLERY Our artillery was much quieter than is usual. At 12 midnight there was	
			a 5 minute bombardment of enemy posts in front of HOLLEBEKE.	
			Hostile Artillery was also quieter than usual - OAF AVENUE, IMPERIAL AVENUE + CHATEAU WOOD	

D. D. & L., London, E.C.
(A7883) Wt. W807/M1672 350,000 4/17 Sch. 52a Forms/C/2118/14

Sheet 7.

Army Form C. 2118.

Instructions regarding War Diaries and Intelligence Summaries are contained in F. S. Regs., Part II, and the Staff Manual respectively. Title pages will be prepared in manuscript.

WAR DIARY
or
INTELLIGENCE SUMMARY.
(Erase heading not required.)

Place	Date	Hour	Summary of Events and Information	Remarks and references to Appendices
LINE	5.1.18		receiving attention	
			A Hostile Trench Mortar bombardment of the HOLLEBEKE district	
			took place from 1.0 p.m. to 1.30 p.m.	
			There was no aircraft activity due to lack of visibility. – occasionally single machines	
			came into view. One Enemy Aircraft was brought down on our left flank.	
LINE.	6.1.18		Fine but dull and cold. Very low visibility. Ground – frozen.	
			On account of the Infantry relief no firing was done by our Machine Guns.	
			Our Artillery was inactive, whilst hostile artillery was also very quiet – about 40 small	
			shells fell in FUSILIER WOOD, CHATEAU WOOD and the CANAL BANK.	
			Aircraft activity below normal. One of our planes was over BATTLE WOOD about	
			3.0 p.m. Three of our planes were observed to be dropping signals over the Enemy lines	
			– signal – a cluster of white lights. Hostile aircraft activity was nil.	
			A new S.O.S. chart was made for No. 14 gun whilst Range Cards were made	
			for No. 13 + Sniping Guns.	
LINE.	8.1.18.		Thaw set in. Ground very wet and soft. Visibility on the whole was very poor.	
			Machine Guns. Our guns fired 8000 rounds on LOCK 4 and Enemy tracks in P.1.8, P.7.c.	

D. D. & L., London, E.C.
(A7883) Wt. W803/M1672 350,000 4/17 Sch. 52a Forms/C/2118/14

Sheet 8.

Army Form C. 2118.

Instructions regarding War Diaries and Intelligence Summaries are contained in F. S. Regs., Part II. and the Staff Manual respectively. Title pages will be prepared in manuscript.

WAR DIARY
or
INTELLIGENCE SUMMARY.
(Erase heading not required.)

Place	Date	Hour	Summary of Events and Information	Remarks and references to Appendices
			I 36 a, O 12 b, P 7 c – no retaliation	
			Artillery. Our artillery was quiet whilst hostile Artillery was quiet. A few shells fell in FUSILIER WOOD, CANAL BANK, RAILWAY EMB^T + SUPPORT LINE.	
			Aircraft. Our planes were active throughout the day. Between 8. pm. and 11-0 pm a large number of aeroplanes crossed the enemy lines.	
			Two hostile planes were observed.	
			No hostile balloons were observed.	
LINE	8.1.18.		A rapid thaw set in and continued throughout the day. Visibility was again only moderate.	
			Machine Guns:- 14000 rounds expended. LOCK 4 and enemy centres of movement received our attention. I.36.d. P.2.c. P.2.b. J.32.d. There was no retaliation.	
			Artillery:- Our artillery was fairly active during the afternoon. but hostile guns were quiet.	
			Aircraft. Our planes were very active during the afternoon – Enemy planes not observed.	

D. D. & L., London, E.C. (A7883) Wt. W80/M1672 350,000 4/17 Sch. 52a Forms/C/2118/14

Sheet 9.

Army Form C. 2118.

Instructions regarding War Diaries and Intelligence Summaries are contained in F. S. Regs., Part II. and the Staff Manual respectively. Title pages will be prepared in manuscript.

WAR DIARY
or
INTELLIGENCE SUMMARY.
(Erase heading not required.)

Place	Date	Hour	Summary of Events and Information	Remarks and references to Appendices
LINE	9.1.18		Snow fell during the early morning and the ground was frozen hard. The visibility was quite good at intervals during the day.	
			Machine Guns:- 12000 rounds were fired by our guns on enemy tracks + centres of movement in O.12.b, O.7.c, I.36.a. P.3.c. P.2.b. J.32.d. Enemy M.G. fire was unusually inactive. Two enemy were observed from our sniping position by means of glasses but the fire was ineffective.	
			Artillery activity on both sides was much below normal. The enemy fired on O11 a + b, WHITE CHATEAU + OAK AVENUE, about 140 rounds of small shell.	
			Aircraft. 3 of our planes were observed at 7.45 am and at at 16.0 hours They were patrolling our lines.	
			No enemy plane was observed and no balloons were observed.	
			At 10.0 am. Smoke was seen to rise from chimneys in WERVICQ.	
			2 boxes of S.A.A. were brought to gun positions from TRANSPORT CORNER – empty boxes returned to DUMP.	

D. D. & L., London, E.C.
(A7883) Wt. W803/M1672 350,000 4/17 Sch. 52a Forms/C/2118/14

Sheet. 10.

Army Form C. 2118.

Instructions regarding War Diaries and Intelligence Summaries are contained in F. S. Regs., Part II, and the Staff Manual respectively. Title pages will be prepared in manuscript.

WAR DIARY
or
INTELLIGENCE SUMMARY.
(Erase heading not required.)

Place	Date	Hour	Summary of Events and Information	Remarks and references to Appendices
LINE.	10.1.18		The ground was soft due to rain and thaw. The visibility was good in the morning but was afterwards bad.	
			Machine Guns. Our guns were far more active than usual on account of our assistance to three raids carried out on our front.	
			12 guns of the Company were in the line – 4 of them occupying previously reconnoitred positions in the shell hole line – near BELGIAN WOOD. Flank barrages were laid down and were carried out according to programme.	
			77,250 rounds were expended during the above mentioned raids	
			4000 – Road from CHATEAU Fm to CHALK Fm.	
			7000 – LOCK 5.	
			16.250 – Tracks in I 36 a. P.2.c. P.1.c. P.8.a.	
			50,000 – Flanks of small raid in front of HOLLEBEKE.	
			One gun was rendered useless by shell fire	
			Casualties L.CPL. C. COOK – KILLED by shell fire.	
			Pte J. COPLESTONE – WOUNDED – – –.	

D. D. & L., London, E.C.
(A7883) Wt. W803/M1672 350,000 4/17 Sch. 52a Forms/C/2118/14

Sheet. 11.

Army Form C. 2118.

WAR DIARY
or
INTELLIGENCE SUMMARY.
(Erase heading not required.)

Instructions regarding War Diaries and Intelligence Summaries are contained in F. S. Regs., Part II. and the Staff Manual respectively. Title pages will be prepared in manuscript.

Place	Date	Hour	Summary of Events and Information	Remarks and references to Appendices
LINE.	10.1.18		The Infantry Raids carried out by the 10th Royal Fusiliers and the Kings Royal Rifles were successful - fairly stiff opposition was encountered.	
			The Enemy laid down a very heavy barrage near BELGIAN WOOD and on our left flank. Casualties were inflicted on the Enemy and two light machine Guns were brought in.	
	11.1.18		Word reached us that we were to be relieved by the Machine Guns of the 4th Australian Division. Arrangements were made, handing over statements prepared and guides were sent to SPOIL BANK to meet the AUSTRALIANS. However owing to some mishap the relief was delayed considerably. About 9.0 pm. the relief commenced and was carried out without a hitch. No casualties. Nos. 1 of all guns were left behind with the Australians for a period of 24 hours.	
			All maps of the sector were handed over.	
			The Transport of the Company left the transport lines under orders of 111th Infantry Brigade and marched to STRAZEELE. where they halted for the night. Hot food was prepared and blankets aired for men coming	

D. D. & L., London, E.C.
(A7883) Wt. W807/M1672 350,000 4/17 Sch. 52a Forms/C/2118/14

Sheet. 17.

Army Form C. 2118.

WAR DIARY
or
INTELLIGENCE SUMMARY.
(Erase heading not required.)

Instructions regarding War Diaries and Intelligence Summaries are contained in F. S. Regs., Part II. and the Staff Manual respectively. Title pages will be prepared in manuscript.

Place	Date	Hour	Summary of Events and Information	Remarks and references to Appendices
BAROSSA CAMP + MOVE TO MILLFONTAINE	12.1.18		The Company reached the Transport lines at 2.15 a.m. and were warned after having had food that they were to move at 9.15 a.m. that morning. Reveille was at 6.30 am. and the Camp was cleaned and handed over to the Australians. A motor lorry arrived at 8.0 am. and was loaded with blankets etc. – a few men being sent in it to prepare our new billet. At 9.15 am the company marched off to DICKEBUSCH STN. – where the Coy entrained. We travelled to EBBLINGHEM and there detrained. A march of 5 kilometres brought us to MILLFONTAINE after travelling via LINDE.	
			The billets were cleaned out and sprayed before the company occupied them.	
do	13.1.18		The greater portion of Sunday was allotted to cleaning up equipment etc and in making the camp more comfortable. Rain fell freely the greater part of the day.	
do	14.1.18		Training Programme carried out – in the afternoon it rained heavily. The G.O.C Division visited the billets.	

D. D. & L., London, E.C.
(A7883) Wt. W803/M1672 350,000 4/17 Sch. 52a Forms/C/2118/14

Sheet, 13.

Army Form C. 2118.

Instructions regarding War Diaries and Intelligence Summaries are contained in F. S. Regs., Part II. and the Staff Manual respectively. Title pages will be prepared in manuscript.

WAR DIARY
or
INTELLIGENCE SUMMARY.
(Erase heading not required.)

Place	Date	Hour	Summary of Events and Information	Remarks and references to Appendices
MILL FONTAINE	14.1.18		Programme of Training carried out. Lieut H.G. Stearns proceeded to the U.K. on leave.	
			A fire picquet was detailed and all fire precautions arranged.	
			The Company played the 8th Bn East Lancashire Regt at football and was decisively beaten by six goals to one.	
	15.1.18		Programme of Training carried out. Lt Col Browne visited the billets. A practice fire alarm carried out.	
MILL FONTAINE	16.1.18 to 31.1.18		Programme of Training carried out. Competitive Sports; - football Cross Country Running etc were indulged in every afternoon.	
			At 2.30 p.m. on the afternoon of the 23rd inst the G.O.C. Division inspected the Company in marching order. Officers chargers were rather a fiasco. The G.O.C. had a consultation with Officers + N.C.O.s and stated :- "The turn out is good but I want a great improvement. I want my Company to be the best Company in France".	

E.H. [illegible] Lieut
31.1.18.

D. D. & L., London, E.C. (A7883) Wt. W803/M1672 350,000 4/17 Sch. 52a Forms/C/2118/14

247 M.G.Coy. PROGRAMME OF TRAINING 13-1-18 TO 19-1-18

DATE	NATURE OF TRAINING						LOCALITY
	8-45. A.M.	9 – 10	10 – 11	11 – 12	12 – 1	2-15 TO DUSK	
13-1-18			DIVINE	SERVICES		FOOTBALL	C. 21. A. 2. 3.
14-1-18	INSPECTION	PHYSICAL TRAINING	INSPECTION OF MOBILISATION EQUIPMENT	IMMEDIATE ACTION	CLOSE ORDER DRILL	COMPETITIVE SPORTS INCLUDING	RANGE – C. 21. C. 5. 2.
15-1-18	"	ELEMENTARY GUN DRILL	FITTING & ADJUSTING OF EQUIPMENT	COM ROUTE	PANY MARCH	FOOTBALL RUNNING	
16-1-18	"	PHYSICAL TRAINING	MECHANISM	CLOSE ORDER DRILL	INDICATION & RECOGNITION OF TARGETS	BOXING WRESTLING	
17-1-18	"	EXTENDED ORDER DRILL ARTILLERY FORMATION	DESCRIPTION & METHOD OF EMPLOYMENT OF A.A. SIGHTS	COMBINED DRILL	STRIPPING	SHOOTING { RIFLE REVOLVER M.G.	
18-1-18	"	REPAIRS & ADJUSTMENTS	GAS DRILL	COM ROUTE	PANY MARCH		
19-1-18	"	PHYSICAL TRAINING	SIGHT SETTING & LAYING	LIMBER DRILL	INSPECTION BY COMPANY COMMANDER		

247 M.G. Coy

PROGRAMME OF TRAINING FOR THE PERIOD 20-1-18 TO 26-1-18

DAYS	NATURE OF TRAINING 9 – 10	10 – 11	11 – 12	12 – 1	AFTERNOON	LOCATION
20-1-18		DIVINE	SERVICES			
21-1-18	PHYSICAL TRAINING	"ERROR OF THE DAY"	CLOSE ORDER DRILL	IMMEDIATE ACTION	COMPETITIVE SPORTS	
22-1-18	CLOSE ORDER DRILL	LECTURE "FIRE ORDERS"	COMPANY	ROUTE MARCH	"	
23-1-18	PHYSICAL TRAINING	VISUAL TRAINING INDIVIDUAL INSTRUCTION IN AUTOMATIC TAPPING	GUN DRILL	CLOSE ORDER DRILL	"	
24-1-18	BELT FILLING	LECTURE DEFINITIONS ETC "CONES OF FIRE" "TRAJECTORY" ETC	MECHANISM	JUDGING DISTANCE FORWARD & LATERAL	"	
25-1-18	LIMBER DRILL	ADVANCED STRIPPING REPAIRS	COMPANY	ROUTE MARCH	"	
26-1-18	PHYSICAL TRAINING	COMBINED DRILL	CLEANING OF GUNS & SPARE PARTS	INSPECTION BY O.C. Coy	"	

[illegible] M.G. Coy PROGRAMME OF TRAINING FOR THE PERIOD 27.1.18 – 2.2.18

NATURE OF TRAINING

DATE	9 – 10	10 – 11	11 – 12	12 – 1	AFTERNOON	LOCATION
27.1.18		DIVINE	SERVICES		FOOTBALL	G.21 a.0.5
28.1.18	MACHINE GUN FIRING COMPETITION	RANGE	B.4.a		D°	
29.1.18	CLOSE ORDER DRILL	INDIRECT FIRE LECTURE	INDIRECT FIRE PRACTICAL	IMMEDIATE ACTION COMPETITION	CROSS COUNTRY RUN	
30.1.18	PHYSICAL TRAINING	LIMBER DRILL	REPAIRS & ADJUSTMENTS	POINTS BEFORE, DURING & AFTER FIRING	FOOTBALL	
31.1.18	MECHANISM	LECTURE ESPRIT de CORPS	COMPANY ROUTE	MARCH	D°	
1.2.18	CLOSE ORDER & RIFLE DRILL	STRIPPING	INDICATION & RECOGNITION OF TARGETS	LECTURE MACHINE GUNS IN OFFENSIVE OPERATIONS	D°	
2.2.18	PHYSICAL TRAINING	COR DRILL	INSPECTION OF BOX RESPIRATOR & P.H. HELMETS GAS DRILL	MARCHING ORDER INSPECTION BY O.C. Coy	D°	

Sheet. 1.

217 M.G. Coy

Army Form C. 2118.

Instructions regarding War Diaries and Intelligence Summaries are contained in F. S. Regs., Part II. and the Staff Manual respectively. Title pages will be prepared in manuscript.

WAR DIARY
or
INTELLIGENCE SUMMARY.
(Erase heading not required.)

Vol 8

Place	Date	Hour	Summary of Events and Information	Remarks and references to Appendices
MILL FONTAINE	1-2-18		Training was carried out every for a period of at least four hours	
	12-2-18		The afternoons were devoted entirely to Recreational Training	
			On the evening of the 10th inst. the Company was provided with a special Dinner and musical evening - as a celebration of Christmas festivities. A pig was purchased, and was killed by the Butchers of the Company. The "Barn Owls" provided the Entertainment. Various Officers were detailed, each to his own work, to assist in ensuring a successful evening. Move orders were issued. - a move to the forward area	
	13-2-18		On the morning of the 13th the Transport moved off from MILL FONTAINE to complete its first stage of its journey to the forward area. It proceeded to STRAZEELE where a halt was made for the night. The Company personnel was making all preparations for its move on the morrow. Parties were detailed to thoroughly clean the Camp. All area stores were collected and displayed in such a manner as to facilitate checking on their being handed over to the incoming unit.	

D. D. & L., London, E.C.
(A7883) Wt. W803/M1672 350,000 4/17 Sch. 52a Forms/C/2118/14

Sheet 2.

Army Form C. 2118.

WAR DIARY
or
INTELLIGENCE SUMMARY.
(Erase heading not required.)

Instructions regarding War Diaries and Intelligence Summaries are contained in F. S. Regs., Part II. and the Staff Manual respectively. Title pages will be prepared in manuscript.

Place	Date	Hour	Summary of Events and Information	Remarks and references to Appendices
Feb. 14.			All area stores were handed over and receipts obtained.	
MILL FONTAINE			At 7.45 a.m. The Company left its billets for EBBLINGHEM RAILWAY STATION where at 11.0 pm it was to entrain. The Company arrived at the station at 10.5 a.m. One Officer Lieut. R.W. Storey and One NCO were sent forward to secure the necessary accomodation for the journey. The train left EBBLINGHEM at 11.20 am.	
			At 2.10 pm. we arrived at DICKEBUSCH and detrained. The whole move was under the orders of the 63rd Inf. Bde.	
			The detraining was followed by a march to the Company's Transport Lines (CHIPPAWA CAMP).	
LINE.	15th	1.30pm	At 1.30 pm. two sections of the Company entrained at RENINGHELST on their journey to the line. They detrained at MANOR HALT and proceeded to the allotted portion of the line NORTH of MENIN ROAD. We then relieved nine guns of the 217 M.G. Coy. The relief was completed without mishap and without any casualties.	

D. D. & L., London, E.C. (A7883) Wt. W807/M1672 350,000 4/17 Sch. 52a Forms/C/2118/14

Sheet 3.

Army Form C. 2118.

Instructions regarding War Diaries and Intelligence Summaries are contained in F. S. Regs., Part II. and the Staff Manual respectively. Title pages will be prepared in manuscript.

WAR DIARY
or
INTELLIGENCE SUMMARY.
(Erase heading not required.)

Place	Date	Hour	Summary of Events and Information	Remarks and references to Appendices
LINE.	16th		Company H.Q. situated at VERBEEK FARM is not a very ideal H.Q.	
			work was commenced on it to render it in a more sanitary	
			condition. Salving of material was carried out and the	
			articles were dumped at the Bn. Dump.	
			The day passed very quietly little or no hostile activity	
			either by plane or artillery.	
			At night our guns carried out the usual harassing fire	
			on enemy tracks and centres of movement. A great deal of	
			time was spent in improving the gun positions and surroundings.	
LINE.	17		Frost during the night. No activity was displayed by the enemy.	
			His artillery fired rapid bursts in salvos. light shells, shrapnel	
			and 4.2s at fairly regular intervals.	
			Our guns fired on the Headquarters at J.22.b. 70.00 & GHELUVELT	Sheet E1.
			CROSS ROADS – 13000 rounds being expended.	
			Hostile Aircraft was very active all day.	
			Work on gun positions was continued.	

D. D. & L., London, E.C.
(A7883) Wt. W603/M1672 350,000 4/17 Sch. 52a Forms/C/2118/14

Sheet 4.

Army Form C. 2118.

WAR DIARY
or
INTELLIGENCE SUMMARY.
(Erase heading not required.)

Instructions regarding War Diaries and Intelligence Summaries are contained in F. S. Regs., Part II. and the Staff Manual respectively. Title pages will be prepared in manuscript.

Place	Date	Hour	Summary of Events and Information	Remarks and references to Appendices
LINE	17		and much salving was done. At the transport lines, CHIPPAWA CAMP two salvage dumps were formed and every hut vacant was searched. A considerable quantity of material was thus salved.	
"	18		Company Headquarters moved from VERBEEK FARM to GLENCORSE WOOD TUNNELS. Rain and thaw rendered the ground very sticky and the going difficult.	
			Artillery activity on enemy approaches, and POLDERHOEK was carried out throughout the day and night. The hostile artillery was quiet. A counter preparation scheme was carried out at 5.30 am.	
			Machine Guns carried out their normal harassing fire. FAIRCOTTS Bn H.Q. J22 b.70.00 + GHELUVELT X roads being engaged. 16000 rounds were expended.	
			Hostile Machine Guns were slightly less active than usual. They swept our duckboard tracks at irregular intervals.	
			Hostile Aircraft was again active throughout the day.	
			- One hostile plane was forced to land behind the enemy lines, apparently	

D. D. & L., London, E.C.
(A7883) Wt. W803/M1672 350,000 4/17 Sch. 52a Forms/C/2118/14

Sheet 5

Instructions regarding War Diaries and Intelligence Summaries are contained in F. S. Regs., Part II, and the Staff Manual respectively. Title pages will be prepared in manuscript.

Army Form C. 2118.

WAR DIARY
or
INTELLIGENCE SUMMARY.
(Erase heading not required.)

Place	Date	Hour	Summary of Events and Information	Remarks and references to Appendices
LINE.	18		having been damaged by our A.A. guns.	
			In the Evening the Enemy put up white lights from POLDERHOEK CHATEAU —	
			No apparent action.	
LINE.	19		The ground was frozen hard and the going good. Both Artilleries	
			were quieter than usual. POLDERHOEK CHATEAU was subjected to bursts of	
			fire. No definite shelling by the Enemy took place.	
			Our Machine Guns were normally active - centres of Enemy movement	
			being Engaged. 5000 rounds were fired.	
			The visibility being only fair aerial activity was below normal.	
			At 7.30 am 3 hostile 'planes were seen flying high on our front.	
			At 6.45 pm one hostile plane flew overhead	
			From 6.0 pm - 6.45 pm. the Enemy fired red and green lights - no apparent	
			action.	
			A new Emplacement was made at the Entrance to the new	
			tunnel about J 14 b. 35. 35.	
LINE.	20		Capt. V A TYLOR began to complain of being unwell.	

D. D. & L., London, E.C.
(A7883) Wt. W803/M1672 350,000 4/17 Sch. 52a Forms/C/2118/14

Sheet 9

Army Form C. 2118.

Instructions regarding War Diaries and Intelligence Summaries are contained in F. S. Regs., Part II. and the Staff Manual respectively. Title pages will be prepared in manuscript.

WAR DIARY
or
INTELLIGENCE SUMMARY.
(Erase heading not required.)

Place	Date	Hour	Summary of Events and Information	Remarks and references to Appendices
LINE.	20		The visibility was very variable but was generally speaking only poor.	
			The ground was frozen by day but at night a thaw set in	
			From 8.0 pm. to 8.30 pm a heavy bombardment was opened out on our right	
			Hostile artillery was inactive - only a few shells being fired on to MENIN ROAD	
			Our Aircraft was active throughout the day - Enemy aircraft inactive	
			Our Machine Guns maintained their nightly harassing fire - tracks	
			in J17 c 10.20 to J17 c 30.18 being engaged. 5,500 rounds expended.	
			A second new emplacement was made at the entrance to the Tunnels	
			about J14.b.3.5.	
	21		The condition of the ground was bad but improving. The visibility	
			was very good + consequently aerial activity was greatly increased	
			Our planes were active throughout the day whilst in addition six	
			hostile planes were observed. - all flying high.	
			The two artilleries were fairly quiet. A German gun (high velocity)	
			fired small shell into J.14. from 10.30 am to 2.0 pm. - about 70 shells	
			In the afternoon the same gun put on to the same area 40 shells.	

D. D. & L., London, E.C.
(A7893) Wt. W803/M1672 350,000 4/17 Sch. 52a Forms/C/2118/14

Sheet: 7

Army Form C. 2118.

Instructions regarding War Diaries and Intelligence Summaries are contained in F. S. Regs., Part II. and the Staff Manual respectively. Title pages will be prepared in manuscript.

WAR DIARY
or
INTELLIGENCE SUMMARY.
(Erase heading not required.)

Place	Date	Hour	Summary of Events and Information	Remarks and references to Appendices
LINE.	21		Two pits were dug to take frames for two "Champagne" emplacements at the mouth of shafts - J.14.b. 3.3.	
"	22		A misty morning with ground muddy on account of the thaw. Aerial activity was below normal. Twelve of our machines were observed during the morning but no enemy plane was observed. Our Artillery bombarded POLDERHOEK CHATEAU and vicinity and probably the whole of the Divisional front from 3.30 am to 4.30 am, and from 5.0 am to 6.0 am. Hostile artillery was inactive. Machine Gun activity was normal. 10,500 rounds were fired on enemy tracks and centres of movement. Inter Company relief. Salvage was continued. Bursting layers were placed over the Tunnel in J.14. Capt. Tylor Evacuated. Lieut. Cunliffe took over Command	
"	23		The morning was showery and very windy - the visibility only fair. The whole day was very quiet. From 9.0 pm - 9.30 pm. and again at 3.30 am - 3.45 am our artillery opened heavily on the Enemy lines on our left.	

D. D. & L., London, E.C. (A7883) Wt. W803/M1672 350,000 4/17 Sch. 52a Forms/C/2118/14

Sheet 8.

Army Form C. 2118.

Instructions regarding War Diaries and Intelligence Summaries are contained in F. S. Regs., Part II. and the Staff Manual respectively. Title pages will be prepared in manuscript.

WAR DIARY
or
INTELLIGENCE SUMMARY.
(Erase heading not required.)

Place	Date	Hour	Summary of Events and Information	Remarks and references to Appendices
LINE	23	7.15 am.	Both sides aerial activity was very little. One hostile aeroplane flying very low was engaged by Machine Gun and Rifle fire and was driven off.	
			MENIN ROAD was swept by Machine Gun fire during the night. 2500 rounds being expended. A hostile M.G. fired over our battery position and also over the duckboard tracks in J15.	
			During our bombardments the Enemy sent up red & yellow lights	
"	24		Visibility was again low whilst the ground was in a very soft condition. Both artilleries were rather active throughout the period under review. At 11.55 pm. the Enemy opened a rather heavy bombardment which was continued until 12.30 a.m. Our Artillery replied very vigorously	
			Our Machine Guns carried out the usual harassing fire throughout the night - Tracks in J17a 10.20 to J17a 50.18 were fired on - 9000 rounds expended.	
			Hostile machine gun fire was also maintained throughout the night - on tracks and over our gun positions.	

D. D. & L., London, E.C. (A7883) Wt. W807/M1672 350,000 4/17 Sch. 52a Forms/C/2118/14

Sheet 9.

Army Form C. 2118.

Instructions regarding War Diaries and Intelligence Summaries are contained in F. S. Regs., Part II. and the Staff Manual respectively. Title pages will be prepared in manuscript.

WAR DIARY
or
INTELLIGENCE SUMMARY.
(Erase heading not required.)

Place	Date	Hour	Summary of Events and Information	Remarks and references to Appendices
LINE.	24		A party of about 16 strong was observed at 9.30 am near POLDERHOEK CHATEAU – they disappeared before fire could be brought to bear on them.	
			A practice relay post S.O.S was carried out. At 8.0 pm. about 20 green lights were observed.	
			One man No GREENHALL was slightly wounded but remained at duty.	
"	25		Rain fell early morning rendering the ground very heavy.	
			The visibility varied considerably during the day – very low in the morning and moderately high during the afternoon.	
			Our Artillery fire was normal – the usual harassing fire & destructive shoots being carried out.	
			Hostile artillery was considerably above normal.	
			BLACK WATCH CORNER TRACK, CARLISLE FARM, VERBEEK FARM received attention from 3.0 pm. and intermittently throughout the night.	
			Our Machine Guns fired 9,500 rounds on tracks J.17.c.30.60, J.27.a.7.3 to C.1.4., COSY COTTS, and JENKINS Fm.	E1

D. D. & L., London, E.C.
(A7883) Wt. W803/M1672 350,000 4/17 Sch. 52a Forms/C/2118/14

Sheet 10.

Army Form C. 2118.

Instructions regarding War Diaries and Intelligence Summaries are contained in F. S. Regs., Part II. and the Staff Manual respectively. Title pages will be prepared in manuscript.

WAR DIARY
or
INTELLIGENCE SUMMARY.
(Erase heading not required.)

Place	Date	Hour	Summary of Events and Information	Remarks and references to Appendices
LINE	25		Usual hostile M.G. fire over tracks + gun positions.	
			Aircraft was generally speaking active throughout the day.	
			A fire was observed in the direction of ZANDVOORDE from 4 – 4.15 p.m.	
			Salvage dumps were made at 18 and 20 positions and Nos 21 + 22 gun positions were cleared of much refuse.	
			No 22 Emplacement was made splinterproof.	
"	26.		The morning was bright and fine: – consequently both artilleries were more than normally active.	
			Throughout the day the tracks were shelled with Shrapnel, 4.2s and 5.9s and during the night VERBEEK FARM was shelled. A few gas shells were sent over by the Enemy.	
			Our Machine Guns were more active than usual. During the day much Enemy movement was reported on SWAGGER FARM. 1000 rounds were expended on this position.	
			Harassing fire was increased during the night 15000 rounds being expended. Tracks J17c 30.70, J18 a, 20.30, J22b 6.0 received attention	

Sheet 11 Army Form C. 2118.

Instructions regarding War Diaries and Intelligence Summaries are contained in F. S. Regs., Part II. and the Staff Manual respectively. Title pages will be prepared in manuscript.

WAR DIARY
or
INTELLIGENCE SUMMARY.
(Erase heading not required.)

Place	Date	Hour	Summary of Events and Information	Remarks and references to Appendices
LINE.	26		A flashlight was seen at 8.15 pm. in direction of ZANDVOORDE	
			— — — 11.15 — — — — GHELUVELT.	
			Emplacement at No. 21 position was improved and the traverse increased. 500 sandbags were drawn and filled for a new emplacement.	
"	27		Visibility was high and artillery activity was maintained. At 4.0 am we put down a barrage on the hostile trenches.	
			The Enemy put down a very heavy barrage on our Sector at 4.0 am and at 1.0 am on the sector to our left.	
			Our machine Guns fired 15000 rounds on tracks J17c, J23a, J22b J28a and on practice S.O.S.	
			Usual Enemy hostility over our tracks + positions	
			Aerial activity was greater than the preceding day.	
			Enemy threw up Double reds, greens + yellow lights during the barrage	
			At 2.50 am flashlight signals were seen in the direction of POLDERHOEK CHATEAU. Considerable work was done during the hours of darkness	

D. D. & L., London, E.C.
(A7883) Wt. W803/M1672 350,000 4/17 Sch. 52a Forms/C/2118/14

Sheet 17.

Army Form C. 2118.

Instructions regarding War Diaries and Intelligence Summaries are contained in F. S. Regs., Part II. and the Staff Manual respectively. Title pages will be prepared in manuscript.

WAR DIARY
or
INTELLIGENCE SUMMARY.
(Erase heading not required.)

Place	Date	Hour	Summary of Events and Information	Remarks and references to Appendices
LINE	28		High visibility with increased Artillery activity.	
			Our Artillery was active during the afternoon on POLDERHOEK CHATEAU 4.0 pm to 5.0 pm. At 3.0 am – 5.30 am fire was maintained on the hostile lines developing into barrage fire from 3.0 am – 3.45 am and from 5.30 am – 5.45 am.	
			The Enemy opened a heavy bombardment on our left, during the night and again after and during our bombardment.	
			At 11.0 pm he fired gas shells close to VERBEEK FM.	
			During the morning he dispersed a ~~he~~ working party.	
			Machine Guns were extremely active. 45,500 rounds being fired on tracks J22d, J18 C, 55 35. and on S.O.S lines in cooperation with Artillery.	
			The 13th R.B. relieved the 10th R.F. Changes were made in the disposition of No 26 gun. The Gun + Crew were transferred from JULE 59-96 to JERK FM. A relay post established between this gun and CARLISLE FARM. A 4 gun battery was formed at VERBEEK FARM	

D. D. & L., London, E.C.
(A7883) Wt. W80/M1672 350,000 4/17 Sch. 52a Forms/C/2118/14

Army Form C. 2118.

Instructions regarding War Diaries and Intelligence Summaries are contained in F. S. Regs., Part II. and the Staff Manual respectively. Title pages will be prepared in manuscript.

WAR DIARY
or
INTELLIGENCE SUMMARY.
(Erase heading not required.)

Place	Date	Hour	Summary of Events and Information	Remarks and references to Appendices
			12 guns complete were now in position and the remaining 4 guns were kept at Coy H.Q. GLENCORSE TUNNELS. A special precaution had been issued and great alertness prevailed. Patrols were very active.	
			Ammunition was disposed of as follows:-	
			i A Company Reserve Dump - situated near to Coy. H.Q.	
			ii A reserve Dump at each battery position, centralised and capable of allowing belt fillers to work under good cover.	
			iii A reserve supply of S.A.A. at each separate gun.	
			All M.G. Headquarters - Company and Section are connected by telephone.	

[illegible] Lieut.
OC 217 M.G. Coy.

(A7883) Wt. W809/M1672 350,000 4/17 D. D. & L., London, E.C. Sch. 52a Forms/C/2118/14

[illegible] Group. in present H.Q. in K.9. under O.C. 4th Aust'n M.G. Coy. Consisting of 10 guns 4th Australian M.G. Coy. disposed as follows:–

2 guns in K.21.
2 guns in K.20.
2 guns in their old positions in K21. C. and K.11.c.
2 guns in K.15.
2 guns in K.8.

Reserve Guns.

"C" Coy. 37th Bn. M.G.C.

4 guns in K.1.a.
2 guns in K.7.c.
8 guns at Transport Lines.

"D" Coy. 37th Bn. M.G.C.

5 guns at Transport Lines.

4th Australian Machine Gun Coy.

6 guns at Transport Lines.

10. "A" Group will be under G.O.C. RIGHT BGDE
"B" Group " " " G.O.C. RIGHT CENTRE BGDE
"C" Group " " " G.O.C. LEFT CENTRE BGDE
"D" Group " " " G.O.C. LEFT BGDE

"D" Group will be prepared for calls from other Brigades through G.O.C. LEFT BGDE.

11. Tripods, Belts etc. will not be taken over or handed over on relief.

12. Range cards, aiming points, fighting maps etc will be handed over on relief.

13. Completion of relief will be notified by wire to the 37th Bn. Machine Gun Corps and Division by the Code Word, APPLES.

14. Acknowledge.

[illegible]
Lieut-Col
Commanding 37th Bn Machine Gun Corps

Issued at 6 a.m. 12-4-18

Copies to.

1. G.O.C. 37th Div.
2. "G" — " —
3. Q — " —
4. 63rd Bgde
5. 112th — " —
6. 111th — " —
7. 4th Aust'n Bgde
8. 4th Aust'n M.G. Coy.
9. A Coy. 37th Bn M.G.C
10. B " — " —
11. C " — " —
12. D " — " —
13. New Zealand Div.
14. — " — M.G. Bn.
15. 62nd Division
16. 62nd — " — M.G. Bn
17. Corps M.G. Off'r.
18. Sig. Supt.
19. Art'y. 37th Div.
20. File
21. War Diary.

www.ingramcontent.com/pod-product-compliance
Lightning Source LLC
Chambersburg PA
CBHW081556160426
43191CB00011B/1946
* 9 7 8 1 4 7 4 5 1 8 1 3 0 *